Master The Uses of Ser & Estar

Samuel Arredondo

www.givemefluency.com

Master The Uses Of Ser & Estar

Copyright © 2020 by Samuel Arredondo

Written by Samuel Arredondo.

2020 Edition

Visit:

www.givemefluency.com

Dedication

For Mr. Geidd, my high school Spanish Teacher.

Master The Uses Of Ser & Estar
Table of Contents

CHAPTER ONE

Why a Book on Ser & Estar?

To Be in Spanish— Easy Peasy
Ser y Estar en Español— Facilísimo

One of the biggest issues I have noticed is that many Spanish language learners have a hard time figuring out when to use the two fundamental and very important verbs, **Ser** and **Estar** (to be), and what the difference is between them. This can be frustrating, especially for someone who is just starting out learning the language.

But it doesn't have to be frustrating!

A perhaps mind-boggling concept that the average Spanish-language learner encounters is the *mystery of Ser and Estar*. The fact is, if he or she is a native English-speaking learner of Spanish, there is only one verb that they use in English to express "to be". In English, we use this verb thousands of times a day without even thinking too much about it:

To Be

I **am**
You **are**
He, she, it **is**
We **are**.
You (all) **are**
They **are**.

Easy peasy. However, in Spanish, there are actually *two* ways to express "to be", which are **"Ser"** and **"Estar"**. In Spanish, each of these two verbs is *conjugated* to reflect the subject of the verb as well as the tense—past, present, future, conditional, etc.

Ser *(to be)*

Yo **soy**
Tú **eres**
Él, ella, usted **es**
Nosotros **somos**
Vosotros **sois**
Ellos, ellas, ustedes **son**

Estar *(to be)*

Yo **estoy**
Tú **estás**
Él, ella, usted **está**
Nosotros **estamos**
Vosotros **estáis**
Ellos, ellas, ustedes **están**

Side Note: The *full verb conjugations* of Ser and Estar are in the back of the book for quick reference.

And since there are two different words used to express "to be" in Spanish, it may seem strange and difficult at the beginning of our language learning journey. But once you get the hang of it, you'll be able to "feel" why Spanish uses the two different verbs. It will just make sense. It will just "feel" right, and if it just so happens that you make a mistake and use the wrong "to be" verb when you're speaking Spanish, you'll realize it… and you'll understand why you realize it.

I hope this makes sense. And if it doesn't, it will by the time you finish this book. For now, take a deep breath, tell yourself it's all gonna be okay, and let's dive in!

What's The Purpose Of This Book?
¿Cuál Es El Motivo De Este Libro?

"Why do I even need this book?"

You may be asking yourself this question. Well, like the rest of us, you may have seen a couple of books floating around out there that deal with the subject of Ser vs. Estar. But I have not seen many books that explain Ser and Estar in sufficient detail, that squash all doubts about their usage, and instill such a sense of confidence in the reader that by the time they complete the book he or she can proudly say, "Hey, I really get it now. Cool!"

Therefore, it is my mission to change this. It is my purpose to write a book that gives us exactly what we need and ends the quest for that missing information in our Spanish learning journey.

By the end of this book, after you have read all the chapters and completed all the exercises, I am confident that you will have mastered the usages of Ser and Estar and will be ready to go out and speak like you know what you're doing.

My Recommendation For The Exercises

The exercises in the sections "*Uses of Ser*" and "*Uses of Estar*" are straightforward— the sentences either use a form of Ser, or a form of Estar. My recommendation is that when you do these exercises, try not to simply fill in the blank with the correct word, but rather utilize a notebook to write out the entire sentences in Spanish with the correct conjugation of Ser or Estar according to the context of the sentence. If you get "stuck", no worries, just check the answers in the back of the book. It's okay to look at the answers in order to get "unstuck", and when you encounter the same sentence later in the book, it will be easier to recall.

You will note that the sentences presented in the exercises are not overly complex, as the point is not to trick you or cause you to fail, but rather to give you the practice you need to become very familiar with the usages of Ser and Estar, hence the recommendation to write out the sentences.

Completing the exercises in this manner will help you accomplish three things:

- By writing the sentences out, you will get used to using Ser and Estar *in its context*.
- By writing the sentences out, it will enable you to easily remember when to use either/or when you *speak* the language.
- This will also help you tremendously when you get to the Final Review, where you will review every sentence that you have practiced so far.

A System That Simply "Makes It Stick"

The book is set up in such a way that it will enable you to remember what you are studying. Let's face it— if we can't remember what we study, would we even study in the first place? Nope. We wouldn't, would we? The verb usages that you will be exposed to, if you do the exercises as explained above, will become easy to remember. And by the end of this book, you'll be very confident in your knowledge of Ser and Estar.

Debunking the Myth of Permanent & Temporary

In the realm of Spanish study, there are lists and lists of rules that are used for helping the language learner understand the difference between **Ser** and **Estar**. Here are a couple of the rules that we have all seen, time and time again:

For anything that is ***permanent***, use **Ser**.

For anything that is ***temporary***, use **Estar**.

There cannot be anything worse than telling this to a Spanish language student. Why? Because the only thing that these rules are going to do is *confuse the heck out of people*. These rules just don't cover everything. For example, look at these two properly written sentences:

El hombre está muerto. (The man is dead.) Is he dead only temporarily? Will he come back to life tomorrow, since this seems to be temporary?

Mi primo es policía. (My cousin is a policeman.) Will he be policeman permanently, forever and ever? What if he decides to switch to become a lawyer instead?

These rules are taught in our schools. They are taught via the Internet on Spanish learning websites. These rules are in the

Spanish grammar books that I have on my bookshelf in my living room. Now, it doesn't have to mean that we can't buy these books and use them. There is certainly some very helpful information in them. I've used them with the concept in mind:

"Eat the meat, spit out the bones."

But why should we have to do that? The authors of these books are simply not telling us the *whole* story about the usages of Ser and Estar. And that's where this book comes in. I want you to know **the whole story** about Ser and Estar.

The "DOCTOR and PLACE" rule is just not good enough.

Here is something that is taught in the Spanish learning world that you may have come across:

"The uses of Ser and Estar can be memorized using the acronyms DOCTOR and PLACE."

Don't get me wrong - acronyms can surely be of some help. But the problem that I have with these two lists is that they are **incomplete**. Here's what I'm talking about, just in case you haven't run into these lists before:

D.O.C.T.O.R.

- Date/Description
- Occupation
- Characteristic
- Time
- Origin
- Relationship

P.L.A.C.E.

- Position
- Location
- Action
- Condition
- Emotion

Placement Test— Prueba de Nivel

It's time to see where you stand when it comes to hitting the mark on the bullseye of Ser and Estar. Here's a short test to get an idea how well you understand how to use these two important Spanish verbs—nothing to stress about. If you do well, it'll give you some confidence that you have been on the right track. If, on the other hand, you don't do so well, no worries. It will just help you understand what you need to work on. And this, after all, is why I have written this book and why you are reading it.

Side Note: Throughout this book, we'll be using various verb tenses of Ser and Estar. Check the conjugation lists in the back of the book if you need help!

¿Estás listo? ¡Empecemos!

*By the way, why did we use **"estar"** here instead of **"ser"**? If you're not sure, don't worry. We'll be covering that later on!*

Exercise 1— Placement Test. *Choose the correct verb.*

1. No me gustan los platos de papel. Me gusta este plato porque _____ de cerámica.
I don't like paper plates. I like this plate because it's made of ceramic.

2. Corea del Sur _____ el lugar más interesante que he visitado.
South Korea is the most interesting place that I have visited.

3. El profesor de matemáticas _____ muy aburrido. No me gusta su clase.
The math teacher es very boring. I don't like his class.

4. ¿Cuál _____ el primer auto que compraste?
What's the first car that you bought?

5. El concierto va a _____ en el parque mañana por la tarde. ¿Vas a ir?
The concert is going to be at the park tomorrow evening. Are you going?

6. No. Él no asiste a una iglesia judía. _____ católico.
No. He doesn't attend a Jewish church. He's Catholic.

7. Mi hermana mayor _____ una persona bien lista.
My big sister is a very smart person.

8. Fui a clase ayer. Yo _____ tan aburrido que tuve que dejar la clase.
I went to class yesterday. I was so bored that I had to leave the class.

9. Voy a comprar todo esto. ¿Cuánto _____? ¿Y a cuánto _____ un kilo de carne de res hoy?
I am going to buy all this. How much is it (the total)? And

how much is a kilo of beef going for today?

      10. ¿Si pudieras _____ una persona famosa por un día, a quién elegirías?
      If you could be a famous person for one day, who would you chose?

      11. Yo _____ a punto de salir a correr.
      I am about to go out to run.

      12. El jefe quería que yo _____ en el trabajo a las seis de la mañana el día siguiente.
      The boss wanted me to be at work at six in the morning the following day.

      13. Alejandro, aunque tú _____ enfermo, vas a ir a la escuela hoy.
      Alejandro, even though you are sick, you are going to go to school today.

      14. La cuchara grande que _____ de plástico _____ allí.
      The big plastic spoon is over there. (the spoon made of plastic)

      15. Si tuvieras mil millones de dólares _____ rico.
      If you had a billion dollars, you would be rich.

      How did you do?

      Check the answers in the back of the book to find out. Remember, even if you did very well, there is always room for improvement and building confidence! Remember—*Practice makes perfect,* and we'll be practicing quite a bit.

CHAPTER TWO

The Past Tense

Which "Was" Do I Use?

Before moving on to the uses of Ser and Estar, I believe that it is important to discuss their proper usage in the past tense. The exercises that you will encounter throughout the book will use the two verbs in the past, present and future. You will see them used in the infinitive form and in several other tenses.

One of the biggest issues that Spanish learners always seem to run into is choosing which "*was*" to use in different situations.

These are the four ways to say "was" in Spanish (listed here in the 3rd person):

Él, ella, usted...

Fue
Era
Estuvo
Estaba

So how do we know which one to use?

Let's take a look at these two tenses: **Preterite** *and* **Imperfect**.

Preterite tense: We use this tense when we can measure the time (one day, three years, seven minutes, etc.). So, we know how long it lasted, or how long it was. It is used to indicate actions that are single events, a completed action, an action that was repeated a specific number of times, or an action that happened during a certain time period with a definite beginning and end. It tells us when an action took place, *specifically*.

In other words, If we can undoubtedly **measure** the time frame, we can use the **Preterite**.

Preterite of Ser: **Fue**
Preterite of Estar: **Estuvo**

Imperfect tense: We use this tense when we can cannot measure the time, for incomplete actions, repeated an unspecified number of times, mental states, or physical conditions. It tells us when an action took place, *in general*.

Imperfect of Ser: **Era**
Imperfect of Estar: **Estaba**

Example 1

*He **was** a carpenter.*

For how long? We don't know the exact amount of time that he was a carpenter, so we will use the **Imperfect**.

And in order to decide if we need to use **Ser** or **Estar** here, we see that ***occupation*** is something that requires the use of **Ser**.

…so we use the **Imperfect** of **Ser**:

Era *carpintero.*

Example 2

*The concert last Saturday **was** awesome!*

The concert is something for which we can measure the time. It had a beginning and an end. It started at 6pm and ended at 10pm. It came. It went. So, we will use the **Preterite**.

It was a planned event, so we will use **Ser**.

*¡El concierto **fue** genial!*

Example 3

*Samuel **was** sad.*

Can we measure the amount of time that he was sad? No. So we will use the **imperfect** tense.

He normally doesn't behave like this. It's only his current condition. So we will use **Estar**.

Samuel **estaba** triste.

Example 4

*He **was** at work for two hours.*

We know how long. So we will use the **Preterite**.

We know where he was, so we know the location (at work). We will use **Estar**.

Él **estuvo** en el trabajo dos horas.

Example 5

The Imperfect of Ser is *always* used to indicate a time in the past.

Eran las dos de la tarde.
It **was** two in the afternoon.

Example 6

The Imperfect can be used when we want to say that we "used to be" something.

Yo **era** profesor.
I **used to be** a teacher.

Once again, here are the four ways to say *"was"*:

Preterite of Ser: **Fue**
Imperfect of Ser: **Era**
Preterite of Estar: **Estuvo**

Imperfect of Estar: **Estaba**

Another Side Note: This is a lot to think about, but it becomes more and more natural as we practice it. In addition, the uses of Ser and Estar in different situations, like events and jobs, will be explained in upcoming sections. You can reference the back of the book for the full past tense conjugations of Ser and Estar before you do these exercises, if you need to.

Exercise 2.

1. Su abuela _____ española.
His grandmother was Spanish.

2. Nosotros _____ en el partido.
We were at the game.

3. Nuestros papás _____ de Guatemala.
Our parents were from Guatemala.

4. Nosotros _____ allí dos días.
We were there for two days.

5. _____ un día muy divertido.
It was a very fun day.

CHAPTER THREE

Uses of "SER"

Uses of Ser— Los Usos de Ser

Now we are going to get down to the nitty gritty. We are going to go through many uses of the verb **Ser**. In short (very short), Ser can most aptly be characterized as a fundamental Spanish verb that is used to express what something is— and the nature of it's being. It is commonly (and accurately) taught that **Ser** is the **essence** of something and **Estar** is the **condition** of something. If you can ask, "What is it?", you can answer using Ser. For example:

¿Qué **es**?
What **is** it?

Es un lápiz.
It**'s** a pencil.

Side Note: The Spanish verb Ser is derived from the Latin word *esse*, which is where we get the word *essence*. Therefore, Ser is used to describe the essence of things.

Some of the uses of Ser that we'll be covering in this section are as follows:

- Nationality And Place Of Origin
- Race
- Profession/Occupation
- Physical Traits
- Personal Characteristics

- Religious Affiliation
- Shapes
- Size
- Materials Things Are Made Of
- Possession
- Ser With The Infinitive
- Time & Date
- Relationships Between People
- Location of Events
- Gender
- Prices of Things Using Ser
- Impersonal Expressions
- Political Affiliation
- Amounts and Numbers
- Predicate Nominatives
- Commands Using Ser

Nationality and Place of Origin—La Nacionalidad y Lugar de Origen

Ser is used to convey one's nationality, place of origin, or belonging to a particular country. People are born into a nationality. Some become citizens of another country and switch nationalities. And some have dual citizenship—but we always use Ser to describe it. It's more permanent than temporary, but don't let these two words, *permanent* and *temporary* throw you off. Just remember that when we are speaking about where people are from or what kind of citizen they are, we use Ser.

Here are some examples:

We use Ser to say "I am from (somewhere)".

Es de Alemania, pero ahora vive aquí en Ecuador.
He **is** from Germany, but now he lives here in Ecuador.

We use Ser when we say "I am (nationality)". (In Spanish, we generally leave the definite article off (un, una) when we say this, unlike in English where we *normally* use "a" or "an".)

Solía **ser** estadounidense. Ahora **es** ecuatoriano.
He used to **be** an American. Now he **is** an Ecuadorian.

Try not to over-think it. Just remember that with nationalities, we use Ser. Here, we see the verb in it's infinitive form: "Ser"="to be".

Para **ser** ciudadano estadounidense, hay que hacer un examen.
In order to **be** a United States citizen, you have to take a test.

It works the same way when we simply want to say that we are from somewhere in general. Not just "countries"…cities, states, planets, wherever.

Yo **soy** de Texas.
I **am** from Texas.

Yo **soy** de Las Cruces, Nuevo México.
I **am** from Las Cruces, New Mexico.

Yo **soy** de un planeta que está muy lejos de la tierra.
I **am** from a planet that is very far from Earth.

Let's get some practice in.

Exercise 3.

1. Ya aprobé el examen, así que ahora _____ ecuatoriano.
I passed the test, so now I am an Ecuadorian.

2. Estamos de vacaciones en Argentina pero _____ de Chile.
We are on vacation in Argentina but we are from Chile.

3. Aquel engeniero _____ del país más extenso del mundo. _____ ruso.
That engineer over there is from the biggest country in he world. He is Russian.

4. Desde que yo era niño, ese anciano ha dicho que _____ danés. Sin embargo, la verdad es que no _____ de Dinamarca.
Since I was a kid, that elderly gentleman has said that he is Danish. Nevertheless, the truth is that he is not from Denmark.

5. El hombre _____ de nacionalidad boliviana.
The man is of Bolivian nationality. (He's Bolivian.)

Race and Ethnicity—La Raza y El Origen Étnico

Race is a beautiful thing. We are all different. We all have some type of story to tell about our ancestors. I, for instance, am all kinds of stuff— Asian and White with a small dash of Latino thrown in for good measure.

Race is defined as a group of persons related by common descent. In Spanish, we use Ser when we speak of race.

Bronislaw **es** eslavo.
Bronislaw **is** Slavic.

Si estás leyendo este libro, apuesto que **seas** humano.
If you are reading this book, I bet you **are** human.

Chang Min **es** asiática y blanca— su madre **es** asiática y su padre **es** blanco.
Chang Min **is** Asian and White— her mother **is** Asian and her father **is** White.

Ethnicity is a group of people that share a common culture, language or religion.

La cantante famosa, Shakira, **es** latinoamericana.
The famous singer, Shakira, **is** a Latin American.

Una persona cuyos orígenes se encuentran en cualesquiera de los pueblos de las Américas **son** amerindios.
A person whose origins are found in any of the people groups of the Americas **are** Amerindians.

 Exercise 4.

27

1. ¿Y tú? ¿Cuál _____ tu raza?
And you? What's your race?

2. Aleki me ha dicho que _____ samoano, pero ya no. No creo que eso sea posible.
Aleki told me that he was Samoan, but not anymore. I don't believe that that's possible.

3. No creemos que aquel predicador _____ sudamericano porque su acento parece _____ europeo, quizás de España.
We do not believe that that preacher over there is South American because his accent seems to be European, perhaps from Spain.

4. Los españoles, los canarios, y los andaluces _____ de la misma etnia.
Spaniards, Canary Islanders and Andalusians are from the same ethnicity.

5. Personas con raíces africanas, nacidas en el continente americano, _____ afroamericanas.
Persons with African roots, born in the American continent, are Afro-Americans.

Profession/Occupation—La Profesión/El Empleo

We all have a profession or occupation. Paid or not. We all do something. Words that explain what we do all have a name— and those names, when said in Spanish, use Ser. Sure, we may switch jobs now and again, but we do not use Estar just because our jobs or professions changed from last week to this week. This is the reason I explained at the beginning of this book that we just cannot trust the acronyms DOCTOR and PLACE 100%. It just doesn't work all the time, does it?

Here are some examples of using Ser when talking about our jobs:

Antonio fue a la universidad muchos años porque siempre quería **ser** abogado. Y ahora lo **es**.
Antonio went to university many years because he wanted to **be** a lawyer. And now he **is** one.

Para **ser** cocinero, hay que saber mucho sobre la gastronomía.
In order to **be** a cook, you have to know a lot about food.

Lourdes no quiere que su hija **sea** recepcionista como ella, sino que **sea** psicóloga.
Lourdes doesn't want her daughter to **be** a receptionist like her, but rather that she **be** a psychologist.

Side Note: You may have noticed that in Spanish we don't always use the indefinite article (un, una) with occupations in Spanish unless we're describing it, specifically, for example:

Él **es** un buen dentista.
He **is** a good dentist.

But if we are just expressing the idea of *what* he is without any additional information, we say:

Él **es** dentista.
He **is** a dentist.

Ella **será** churrera durante toda su vida porque no sabe hacer nada más.
She **will be** a churro maker her whole life because she doesn't know how to do anything else.

Another Side Note: If someone is in a job temporarily, we can use this expression with Estar:

Estar de + job.

In the following example, we are talking about the fact that Adrian normally works as a translator, but he has been working as a waiter for the last two weeks to make ends meet:

Adrián **está de** camerero ahora, pero ya sabemos que **era** traductor.
Adrian **is working as a** a waiter right now, but we know he **was** a translator.

Let's get some practice done to get this stuff to "stick".

Exercise 5. *Be sure to use the correct verb tense or form of the verb.*

1. Mi abuelo ha _____ un buen relojero durante la mayoría de su vida.
My grandfather has been a good watchmaker for most of his life.

2. Mis amigos que viven en Los Ángeles _____ jardineros paisajistas.

My friends that live in Los Angeles are landscape gardeners.

3. Él trabaja con armas. _____ soldado.

He works with weapons. He is a soldier.

4. El músico pasa su tiempo libre ayudando a otros porque _____ pacifista.

The musician spends his free time helping others because he is a pacifist.

5. Para _____ urólogo, hay que saber mucho sobre la medicina.

To be a urologist, you have to know a lot about medicine.

Physical Traits—Rasgos Físicos

Whether we want to say someone is big, tall, short, small, chunky, skinny, fat, muscular, weak, pretty or pretty ugly— We use Ser to describe physical traits of people in Spanish. Yes, it is possible that physical traits can change— and that is why we have to try to forget the misleading rule of "Ser=permanent" and "Estar=temporary", because, again, it doesn't always work. In Spanish, we use Ser for physical descriptions that describe the *essence* of someone, or the *"what is"* someone.

Look at the difference between these two sentences:

Juan siempre **ha sido** gordo. (Ser)
Juan **has** always **been** fat.

Juan **está** gordo hoy. (Estar)
Juan **is** fat today. (Juan looks fat today)

To explain this further, if we use Estar to say that Juan is fat today, it's more like saying he *looks* fat today. Today is a specific time, as opposed to yesterday, so we use Estar instead. He may not always be fat. Maybe he is an older, thin gentleman who bloats easily and he has just eaten a big bowl of oatmeal. He is generally skinny. He ate too much oatmeal, he is now bloated, and his wife takes a look at him and jokingly (but lovingly) says:

Te he dicho que no comas tanta avena. ¡**Estás** gordo ya!
I have told you not to eat so much oatmeal. You**'re** fat now!

But when we express that someone *is something* (a character, essence, or trait), we use Ser:

*Mike **es** grande.*
*Mike **is** big.*

*Sally **es** baja.*
*Sally **is** short.*

*Mrs. Taylor, the math teacher, **is** thin.*
*La Sra. Taylor, la profesora de matemáticas, **es** delgada.*

Así que en español diríamos frases como estos dos Mexicanos:

— ¡Órale! Mira a aquel güey. ¡**Es** altísimo!
Wow! Look at that dude over there. He **is** super tall!

— ¡No, hombre! Para mí, no **es** tan alto. Es que tú **eres** demasiado bajo. Por eso piensas así.
Nah, man! To me, he **is** not that tall. It's that you **are** too short. That's why you think that.

When asking a question about how someone is, or what he is like, we would say:

Y Arturo, ¿cómo **es**? (or ¿Qué tal **es**?) **Es** muy guapo.
And what about Arturo? What **is** he like? He **is** very handsome.

 Side Note: Later on in this book we will discuss how using Estar instead of Ser to describe physical traits actually can denote another meaning of the words we use to describe people. Don't worry too much about this right now. We'll be covering this in the section called "*Ser/Estar Can Change the Meaning*".

Let's get some good ol' practice in!

Exercise 6.

1. Raúl, según su hermana Carmen, siempre ha _____ gordo y feo.

Raúl, according to his sister Carmen, has always been fat and ugly.

2. Rebeca nunca va a la playa— ella sólo _____ una persona naturalmente bronceada.

Rebecca never goes to the beach— she is just a naturally tanned person.

3. La Señora Madrigal _____ vieja y bizca.

Mrs. Madrigal is old and cross-eyed.

4. El niño, que se llama Hernán, _____ pelirrojo. Pero a él no le gusta porque quisiera tener el pelo moreno.

The boy, who is named Hernán, is a read-head. But he doesn't like it because he would like to have dark hair.

5. El atleta del dibujo de arriba _____ fuerte, pero el enano también _____ relativamente fuerte.

The athlete in the drawing above is strong, but the dwarf is also relatively strong.

Personal Characteristics That Do Not Generally Change—Características Personales Que Normalmente No Cambian

Personal characteristics are what someone is like, how or what somebody is— the essential qualities that define a person. We call these *permanent traits*. These qualities most likely will not change. They can be a name or a physical description. This is sort of close to what we discussed in the previous section, but here we are mainly talking about how the person, animal, or any living creature, is, which describes their character, such as: mean, jealous, grumpy, friendly, cordial, diplomatic, intelligent— in other words, his or her personality. For example:

No me gusta ir a la casa de Alejandro, porque su gato **es** muy malvado. Así **es** el gato.
I don't like to go to Alejandro's house, because his cat **is** very evil. That's how the cat **is**.

Los funcionarios de esta empresa **son** un poco malhumorados y por eso su negocio está sufriendo.
This company's officials **are** a bit grumpy and because of that their business is suffering.

If we were to describe the company's officials' character at any given time, we would say that they are grumpy.

No **seáis** desagradecidos con vuestros padres.
Don't **be** ungrateful to your parents.

If we were to describe these children and how they always are with their parents, we would say that they are ungrateful.

Side Note: Describing characteristics doesn't have to only be about people. We also use Ser when describing other things' general characteristics:

El aire fresco **es** una característica de este pueblo.
The fresh air **is** a characteristic of this town.

In this town, we can always find fresh air. The weather is always good here. The town is known for its good weather and fresh air. These are characteristics of this town.

Talking About Age

We use Ser when we speak about age because age is a characteristic, even though age is constantly changing. Many students or self-studiers learning Spanish are programmed into following the rule that Ser is permanent and Estar is temporary. Talking about age is just another example of why this rule doesn't always apply properly. Look at these sentences:

Javier **es** joven. Pero su abuelo **es** viejo.
Javier **is** young. But his grandpa **is** old.

El abuelo de Javier, cuando **era** joven, solía jugar a béisbol profesionalmente.
Javier's grandfather, when he **was** young, used to play baseball professionally.

Do you see how we used Ser to describe the grandfather's changing age? Ser is used to describe age because it describes the person's essence, even though next year his essence will change.

Side Note: Take a look at the below sentence. If

we say Juanita *looks* young (when we know she is actually old), we would use Estar. That's because we are not describing her essence, but rather how she appears at a specific time.

Juanita se maquilló. ¡Qué joven **está** ahora!
Juanita put some makeup on. How young she **looks** now!

We will cover more of this use of Estar in the section called *"The Intentions Of The Speaker"*.

 Exercise 7.

1. Sus consejos le ayudaron a enderezar la dirección de la empresa. Él _____ un jefe muy sabio.
His advice helped them straighten out the direction of the company. He is a very wise boss.

2. Alberto _____ presentuoso. Cree que hace todo mejor que nadie.
Alberto is arrogant. He thinks he does everything better than anyone.

3. Ella _____ una mujer muy superficial. Lo que dice me aburre.
She is a very superficial woman. What she says bores me.

4. Te dije que mi primo _____ de poca confiaza y tú no me lo creíste.
I told you that my cousin was untrustworthy and you did not believe me.

5. Donald Trump no es político. Sin embargo, _____ una persona carismática, y lo bueno es que sabe mucho acerca de los negocios.
Donald Trump is not a politician. However, he is a charismatic person, and the good thing is that he knows a lot about business.

Religious Affiliation—Afiliación Religiosa

Ser is used to describe what religion one is affiliated with. Plain and simple.

For example:

El cristianismo es la religión oficial de muchos países, pero hay todavía muchas personas que no **son** cristianas.
Christianity is the official religion of many countries, but there are still many people that **are** not Christians.

Las personas que son miembras del movimiento religioso inspirado por la película "La Guerra De Las Galaxias" **son** jedistas.
People who are members of the religious movement inspired by the movie "Star Wars" **are** Jedi.

 Exercise 8.

1. Francisco _____ muy católico. Algún día quere ser el Papa.
Francisco is very catholic. Some day he wants to be the Pope.

2. Para algunas personas, el ateísmo se considera una religión. Para _____ ateo, no es necesario creer en un dios.
To some people, atheism is considered a religion. In order to be an atheist, it is not necessary to believe in a god.

3. Ella _____ budista cuando vivía en Corea de Sur pero ahora _____ cristiana.
She was a Buddhist when she lived in South Korea, but now she is a Christian.

4. El niño me preguntó "¿Qué significa creer en Dios, y por

qué debo _____ cristiano?"…pero yo no sabía la respuesta.
    The boy asked me, "What does it mean to believe in God, and why should I be a Christian? …but I didn't know the answer.

    5. Ellos _____ los musulmanes radicales que vimos ayer en las noticias, los cuales no dejaron a los cristianos sonar las campanas el domingo diciendo que es una falta de respeto a las comunidades musulmanes. No todos los musulmanes son así.
    They are the Radical Muslims that we saw on the news yesterday, which did not let the Christians sound their church bells on Sunday, saying that it is a lack of respect to the Muslim communities. Not all Muslims are like that.

Shapes—Formas y Figuras

Triangles, squares, rhombuses, ovals, octagons— they are all shapes. When we simply want to say that something is a certain shape we would use **Ser** and say:

La forma de la pantalla de la televisión **es** un rectángulo.
The shape of the television screen **is** a rectangle.

Pretty simple, right? And if we say that the TV is "rectangular", as in "rectangle shaped" (adjective), we also use Ser:

La pantalla de la televisión **es** rectangular.
The television screen **is** rectangular.

It is also common to say:

La pantalla de la televisión **es** de forma rectangular.
The television screen **is** rectangle-shaped.

Simply put— if you use Ser for shapes, you'll be safe.

Let's try some more sentences.

 Exercise 9.

1. La forma de la luna en el cielo se llama "círculo". La luna _____ un círculo.
The shape of the moon in the sky is called a "circle". The moon is a circle.

2. La parte superior de la mesa _____ cuadrada.
The top of the table is square.

3. La parte inferior del barco _____ curvo.
The bottom part of the boat is curved.

4. El anillo de plata giró en el aire. El hecho de que el anillo
_____ redondo decidió cómo iba a aterrizar.
The silver ring swung in the air. The fact that the ring was
round determined how it would land.

5. El trozo de queso _____ triangular.
The piece of cheese was triangular.

Sizes—Los Tamaños

Ser is used in Spanish to talk about anything that has to do with size— big, small, medium, large, narrow, wide, deep, shallow… you get the picture. You will see that there are different ways of talking about sizes, but either way you will use Ser.

Side Note: Of course there will be exceptions for different situations in which using Estar instead will change the intent of the speaker. This usage of Estar will be explained more in the section *"Ser/Estar Can Change the Meaning"*.

Look at these examples:

¡Mira! El tamaño del perro **es** menor al tamaño de la botella de agua.
Look! The size of the dog **is** less then the size of the bottle of water.

Espero que el viaje no **sea** muy largo porque no tenemos nada de agua.
I hope the trip **is**n't long because we don't have any water.

Este vestido **es** muy corto para mí.
This dress **is** too short for me.

Time for more practice. ¡Genial!

Exercise 10.

1. La niña quiere ser policía cuando _____ grande.
The girl wants to be a police officer when she grows up

Master The Uses Of Ser And Estar

(when she is big).

2. ¿Cuál es el país más grande del mundo? Rusia
_____ el más grande, ¡y _____ demasiado grande!
What is the biggest country in the world. Russia es the biggest, and it's too big!

3. Este celular _____ muy grande para mi mano. ¿Tiene usted otro más pequeño?
This cell phone is very big for my hand. Do you have a smaller one?

4. El agua en este lugar solía _____ muy profundo, pero ya no.
The water in this place used to be very deep, but not anymore.

5. Además, los niveles de pobreza extrema entre los padres solteros en los Estados Unidos _____ de gran tamaño.
Furthermore, levels of deep poverty among single parents in the United States are of great size.

Materials—Los Materiales

What is something made of? What materials were used to make it? And how do we express this in Spanish? This one can be tricky and the lines between Ser and Estar can get blurry here, so take your time trying to understand it. But don't worry, it's not the end of the road, it's just a bump in the road— a little one that we will be able to easily and briskly jump over with practice!

If we want to say that "something **is** made of" (noun, specifically the name of the material), we can use the construction *es + de*. For example:

¿De qué material **es** esa silla?
What material **is** that chair made of?

Es de madera.
It **is** made of wood.

On the other hand, if we are saying that the thing that was made was a result of an action, we can use Estar. Let's look at this sentence about making a chair:

Hacer una silla es un poco difícil.
Making a chair is a little difficult.

Upon reading the next sentence, we can picture a woodworker with his tools and some wood, putting together a chair with glue and nails— then, sanding and varnishing it.

La silla **está** hecha de madera.
The chair **is** made of wood.

Here, we have made an adjective from the word "hacer", which became "hecha". So then when we put it all together, we get:

¿De qué material **es** esa silla? Pues, **está** hecha de madera.

44

What material **is** the chair made of. Well, it **is** made of wood.

But to make it easy on ourselves, we can simply say:

Es de madera.
(Literally) It **is** of wood.

Yeah. Let's stick with that for now. Hopefully this made it clear, but we will get into some more details in regards to "results of an action" in the section conveniently called "Results of an Action". For now, let's practice some simple "*made of*" sentences.

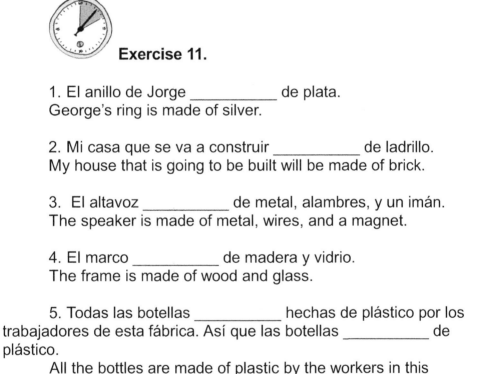

Exercise 11.

1. El anillo de Jorge _____ de plata.
George's ring is made of silver.

2. Mi casa que se va a construir _____ de ladrillo.
My house that is going to be built will be made of brick.

3. El altavoz _____ de metal, alambres, y un imán.
The speaker is made of metal, wires, and a magnet.

4. El marco _____ de madera y vidrio.
The frame is made of wood and glass.

5. Todas las botellas _____ hechas de plástico por los trabajadores de esta fábrica. Así que las botellas _____ de plástico.
All the bottles are made of plastic by the workers in this factory. So the bottles are made of plastic.

Possession—La Posesión

First, a bit of history:

When my big sister and I were kids, we really didn't fight over stuff. She had her Barbie doll and I had my Darth Vader action figure. We really didn't like a lot of the same toys, which made it easy for our parents, right? But I did have a "friend" years later who had the bad habit of taking my things and hiding them. One year, my sister had given me a set of 4 *Matchbox* cars. If you don't know what these are, they're small die-cast cars that came in a little box when you bought them. It turns out that my friend had stolen my cars and buried them in his front yard somewhere. Unfortunately for me, I never found them. *The were mine.* Not his. *Mine.* I had possession of them, then *he* took possession of them. I never saw them again.

Give me a minute to gather myself…

I don't think I ever told my sister about this. But I'm sure she knows now, since she has copy of this book. And so my sad story brings us to how we use Ser to describe owning stuff, like Matchbox cars. Here's what I mean:

¡Este animal de peluche **es** mío! ¡A que no, **es** mío!
This stuffed animal **is** mine! Uh-uh, it's mine!

Yep. This one's easy to remember, because we will **never** say *está mío.* That's just weird.

 Exercise 12.

1. Este concepto no _____ mío, sino que ha sido

acuñado por el Sr. Suárez.
   This concept is not mine, but rather has been coined by Mr. Suárez.

   2. Mi amado _____ mío, y yo _____ suya.
   My beloved is mine, and I am his.

   3. Todos los juguetes debajo de la cama _____ de mi cachorro.
   All the toys under the bed are my puppy's.

   4. La canción popular que le gusta a Amanda se llama "La Fiesta _____ De Nosotros".
   The popular song that Amanda likes is called "The Party Is Ours".

   5. Mi casa _____ su casa.
   My house is your house.

Ser With The Infinitive—Ser y El Infinitivo

Upon reading the title of this section, you might be wondering why the use of Ser with other infinitive verbs would even be mentioned. It would seem to be a very simple and easy to understand concept. You may think this, but the guy next to you, perhaps the absolute beginner, may not. …And for the sake of being thorough with the goal of ensuring that nothing is left out, we will talk about this simple usage of Ser.

Let's talk a bit about what we call the ***infinitive***. It is the completely unconjugated form of the verb. In English, it is "to" plus the "dictionary form" of the verb:

To be
To create
To break
To cry
To live

In Spanish, verbs in the infinitive form carry the endings: **-ar**; -**er**; or **ir**:

Ser/Estar
To be

Crear
To create

Quebrar
To break

Llorar
To cry

Vivir
To live

We can use Ser with other infinitives in this way:

48

Infinitive form of verb + Ser = something or someone or another infinitive

Llegar a tiempo **es algo** muy importante. ->*Llegar es algo*
Arriving on time **is something** very important. ->*Arriving is something*

With another infinitive:

Escribir **es** vivir.
To write **is** to live.

Hacer ejercicio por la mañana temprano puede **ser** una excelente opción.
Exercising in the early morning can **be** an excellent choice.

Basically, if doing something **IS** something, use Ser.

Ser sabio **es** vivir y experimentar.
To be wise **is** to live and experience.

A common expression that is used is:

Es decir…
That **is** to say…

Mi perro es diferente, **es** decir, es un perro raro.
My dog is different, that **is** to say, he is a rare dog.

Very simple, right? …But worth mentioning. Vamos a practicar un poco…

 Exercise 13.

1. Según Álex, _____ músico famoso _____

tener una vida muy ocupada mientras ganas mucho dinero.
According to Alex, being a famous musician is having a really busy life while you earn a lot of money.

2. Beber demasiado alcohol _____ peligroso.
Drinking too much alcohol is dangerous.

3. _____ estúpido no es aconsejable.
Being stupid is not advisable.

4. Disparar un arma _____ un arte en ese país en ese período.
Shooting a gun was an art in that country during that period.

5. Estudiar este libro _____ algo que te ayudará mucho con los verbos Ser y Estar.
Studying this book is something that will help you a lot with the verbs Ser and Estar.

Time and Date—La Hora y La Fecha

Expressing the date and time in Spanish is fairly simple. I realize that on many websites and in some books, we see the writer or teacher talking about how "tricky" it is to talk about the date and time in Spanish. In my experienced opinion, it's really not that tricky. *Really.*

Here are some common ways to ask "What's the date?" in Spanish:

¿Cuál **es** la fecha?
What **is** the date?

¿Qué fecha **es** hoy?
What **is** the date today?

Es el primero de agosto.
It **is** August 1st.

We also use Ser to ask what *day* it is:

¿Qué día **es** hoy?
What day **is** today?

Hoy **es** Sábado.
Today **is** Saturday.

Or simply:

Es Sábado.
It **is** Saturday.

…and what time it is:

¿Qué hora **es**?
What time **is** it?

Son las once.
It **is** eleven o'clock.

We also use Ser when marking a certain period of time.

Es de día.
It **is** daytime.

El espectáculo va a **ser** sólo de día.
The show is going to **be** only during the daytime.

¿**Es** de noche? No. **Es** de día.
Is it nighttime? No. It **is** daytime.

Side Note: Also common in Spanish is a phrase that uses Estar to say or ask what day or date it is: *Estamos a,* literally *"We are at…".* If you think of it as *being in a state of Tuesday* (because tomorrow will be Wednesday), it may be easier to remember.

Estamos a martes.
It **is** Tuesday.

Estamos a lunes, 22 de agosto.
It **is** Monday, August 22nd.

Es domingo.
It **is** Sunday.

Estamos a domingo.
It **is** Sunday.

Literally: We are at Sunday. Expressions like these we just have to memorize. But this one's easy, as it is commonly used!

Exercise 14.

1. Mañana va a _____ mi cumpleaños.
Toworrow's going to be my birthday.

2. Ayer _____ martes.
Yesterday was Tuesday.

3. Ahora _____ la una y media.
Right now it's one thirty.

4. _____ a viernes.
It is Friday.

5. _____ la una y cuarto.
It's 1:15.

Relationships Between People—Las Relaciones Entre Las Personas

We use Ser to describe relationships between people whether they are alive, dead, in a current romantic relationship, or even after someone breaks up.

Ella **es** mi esposa.
She **is** my wife.

Él solía **ser** mi novio.
He used to **be** my boyfriend.

Mara no **es** mi hermana. **Es** mi prima.
Mara **is**n't my sister. She**'s** my cousin.

El señor de esta foto falleció en 1949. Él **es** mi bisabuelo.
The gentleman in this photo died in 1949. He **is** my great-grandfather.

Somos amigos desde hace muchos años.
We **have been** friends for many years.

 Side Note: We will get into detail about someone's actual civil status (married, divorced, single, etc.) in the section *"Civil State"*.

Exercise 15.

1. La mujer está al lado de la niña. La mujer _____ la madre de la niña.
The lady is beside the girl. The lady is the girl's mother.

2. Melodía _____ mi mamá.
Melody is my mother.

3. Luz _____ mi ex-novia.
Luz is my ex-girlfriend.

4. Mi hermana dará luz a un bebé el próximo mes.
_____ mi sobrino.
My sister will have a baby next month. He will be my
nephew.

5. Mi jefe, José Cambián, _____ el primo del rey de
España.
Mi boss, José Cambián, is the cousin of the king of Spain.

Location Of Events Or Occurrences— Ubicación De Los Eventos O Acontecimientos

We know that there are many rules in Spanish, and with those rules come exceptions. Estar is used when we talk about location, but we use Ser when we speak of *where and when* an event takes place.

As long as you can remember what an **event** is and associate it with the verb Ser, this will be a piece of cake! What are events? Well, you know…

Sports/Games/Matches
Parties
Concerts
Presidential debates
Church services
Potlucks
Graduations
Weddings
Award ceremonies

I think you get the picture…

Again, we use Ser to tell *where* an event takes place and *when* an event takes place. For example:

El juego de fútbol **será** en el estadio Santiago Bernabéu.
The soccer game **will be** at the Santiago Bernabéu stadium.

La Convención Nacional Republicana **fue** en Cleveland, Ohio este año.
The Republican National Convention **was** in Cleveland, Ohio this year.

Las vacaciones no **son** en marzo. **Son** en noviembre y

diciembre.

The holidays **are** not in March. They **are** in November and December.

Ser is used to show where or when an event will be held, but if Estar is used, it can change the meaning. Compare these two sentences:

El examen generalmente **es** en la clase grande.
The exam **is** usually in the large classroom. (The exam **is** usually **held** in the large class room.)

El examen generalmente **está** en la clase sobre el escritorio de enfrente, hasta que lleguen los estudiantes.
The exam **is** usually in the class room on the desk in front until the students arrive. (The exam, meaning the actual papers, **is located** on the desk. This is not an event.)

 Exercise 16.

1. El concierto _____ en el Teatro de Luz mañana a las seis en punto. (ser/estar)
The concert will be at the Teatro de Luz tomorrow at six o'clock sharp.

2. La computadora _____ sobre el escritorio. (ser/estar)
The computer is on the desk.

3. La boda _____ en la sala de conferencia de ese edificio.(ser/estar)
The wedding will be in the conference hall of that building.

4. El vestido que la novia va a usar _____ en la sala de conferencia de ese edificio. (ser/estar)
The dress that the bride is going to use is in the conference hall of that building.

5. El juego de fútbol _____ en el estadio que _____ en el centro de la ciudad. (ser/estar)

The soccer game will be held in the stadium that is in the center of the city.

Gender—El Género

We use Ser when speaking of gender, for example:

Mi perro **es** macho
My dog **is** a male.

Y este perro **es** hembra. (Es perra.)
And this dog **is** a female.

Whether it's animals or people we are talking about in regards to gender, we use Ser either way.

Los atletas que acaban de ganar el partido **fueron** todos hombres.
The athletes that have just won the game **were** all men.

Pero creo que las que jugaron luego **fueron** mujeres.
But I believe the ones that played afterward **were** women.

Aquella persona **es** mujer, aunque parezca hombre.
That person over there **is** a lady, even though she looks like a man.

¿Este bebé **es** mujer o hombre?
Is this baby a boy or a girl?

La víctima del accidente **fue** un niño.
The victim of the accident **was** a boy.

 Exercise 17.

1. Cuando _____ niño, fue mi elección caminar sólo a la escuela.

When I was a child, it was my choice to walk to school alone.

2. Yo sí recibí clases de guitarra cuando _____ niña.
I took guitar classes when I was a girl.

3. Estoy mirando estas tarántulas pequeñas, y es casi imposible saber quién _____ macho y quién _____ hembra.
I am looking at these small tarantulas and it is almost impossible to know which is a male and which is a female.

4. La mujer se enfadó y dijo en voz alta "¡Si yo _____ hombre vosotros me habríais dado este trabajo!"
The woman got angry and said aloud "If I were a man you would have given me this job!"

5. ¿Te importa si el médico _____ hombre o mujer? Bueno, pues.
Do you care whether the doctor is a man or a woman? Okay, then.

Prices—Los Precios

We generally use Ser when speaking about how much something costs or what something is valued at. In Spanish we can use the verb "costar", which literally means "to cost". But if we want to simply ask "How much **is** it?" — we can use Ser. We use Ser when we say or ask if something is worth a certain amount, expensive, cheap, or free. For example:

¿Cuánto **es**?
How much **is** it?

Este vestido se ve bonito. ¿Cuánto **es**?
This dress looks nice. How much **is** it?

Es barato. Cuesta diez dólares.
It **is** cheap. It costs ten dollars.

¿Y cuánto **son** estos calzones? Pues esos, como son sucios, **son** gratis.
And how much **are** these underwear? Well those, since they are dirty, **are** free.

Side Note: We will cover more about prices and the uses of Estar in some expressions regarding prices and value in the section "*Prices Using Both Ser and Estar.*"

Exercise 18.

1. ¿En dólares cuánto _____?
How much would it be in dollars?

2. El amor no _____ barato. Cuesta mucho… y a veces, demasiado.

Love is not cheap. It costs a lot… and at times, too much.

3. El juez te dirá cuánto _____ el valor de la multa.

The judge will tell you the amount of the fine. (The judge will tell you how much the amount of the fine is.)

4. ¿Compraste un coche nuevo? ¿Cuánto _____?

You bought a new car? How much was it?

5. Quisiera saber cuánto _____ este libro con el descuento. Sale a €9.55.

I would like to know how much this book will be with the discount. It comes out to €9.55.

Impersonal Expressions—Expresiones Impersonales

Impersonal expressions are sentences or phrases that do not have a specific subject when speaking about something that is taking place. In Spanish, we use Ser for these types of expressions.

For example, in English we say:

It **is** easier to go to the store early in the morning.

In this sentence, the verb is "is" and the subject is "it", but there is no specific subject that "it" refers to. Just "it". What is "it"? It's just a place holder in English, a pronoun for a non-existent subject, if you will. And in Spanish, we would say the sentence like this:

Es más fácil ir a la tienda por la mañana temprano.
It **is** easier to go to the store early in the morning.

In Spanish, it becomes clear what the subject is. The infinitive form of the verb is the subject.

The commonly used construction is simply:

Form of Ser + adjective + the infinitive

Here are some examples of impersonal expressions in Spanish:

Es bueno asistir a la iglesia.
It **is** good to attend church.

Sería malo pegar a otra persona mientras estés enojado.
It **would be** bad to hit another person while you are angry.

Es fácil cumplir con las reglas con tal de que seas una

buena persona.

It **is** easy to follow the rules as long as you are a good person.

Va a **ser** difícil hacer tortillas como las de mi abuela. Sin embargo, lo voy a intentar.

It is going to **be** difficult to make tortillas like my grandma's. Nevertheless, I will try.

Impersonal expressions are also seen with the Spanish subjunctive. The construction is different:

Form of Ser + adjective + the subjunctive form of the verb

Es lógico que se comporte así.

It **is** logical for him to behave like that.

Era imprescindible que lo hicieras como te dije.

It **was** essential that you did it like I told you.

We also see it with **"if"** sentences:

Será interesante *si* el candidato gana la presidencia.

It **will be** interesting *if* the candidate wins the presidency.

Sometimes we use a noun instead of an adjective:

Form of Ser + a noun + subjunctive

Es una lástima que ustedes lleguen tarde.

It **is** a shame that you guys are late.

 Exercise 19.

1. _____ importante saber leer porque te ayudará mucho durante tu vida.

It is important to know how to read because it will help you a lot throughout your life.

2. _____ una lástima que no existan más posibilidades para tener éxito.

It is a pity that there are not more opportunities to succeed.

3. _____ necesario trabajar duro para vivir bien. Así que eso es lo que hice.

It was necessary to work hard in order to live well. So that is what I did.

4. _____ interesante ver la nueva película.

It is going to be interesting to see the new movie.

5. _____ ridículo que ellos fueran al restaurante esta noche en vez de ir a la boda de su hermana.

It would be ridiculous for them to go to the restaurant tonight instead of going to their sister's wedding.

Political Affiliation—Afiliación Política

In Spanish, Ser is used to express a person's or a group's political affiliation.

El Sr. Barnabé dice que **es** republicano.
Mr. Barnabé says he **is** a Republican.

Sin embargo, el Sr. Valdez nos está diciendo que el Sr. Barnabé no puede **ser** republicano verdadero porque no muestra valores republicanos.
Nevertheless, Mr. Valdez is telling us that Mr. Barnabé cannot **be** a true republican because he does not display republican values.

Estos dos candidatos **son** republicanos, pero el tercer candidato **es** demócrata.
These two candidates are republicans, but the third candidate **is** a Democrat.

"Podemos" **ha sido** el cuarto partido más votado de España empezando desde 2014.
"Podemos" **has been** the fourth most voted-for party in Spain beginning from 2014.

Practiquemos un poco…

 Exercise 20.

1. Fue lo que hizo él cuando _____ presidente, hace diez años.

That is what he did when he was president 10 years ago.

2. Si _____ presidente de Ecuador ¿cuál sería tu primera decisión?

If you were president of Ecuador, what would be your first decision?

3. Antes de que ganara esa elección, _____ gobernador de Texas durante cuatro años.

Before he won that election, he was governor of Texas for 4 years.

4. Rita Barbera _____ la alcaldesa de Valencia, España entre 1991 y 2015.

Rita Barbera was the mayor of Valencia, Spain from 1991 to 2015.

5. Hay gente que considera al papa una figura política de europea. Sin embargo, no _____ un político sino un líder religioso.

There are those who consider the Pope a political figure. Nevertheless, he is not a politician but rather a religious leader.

Amounts and Numbers—Cantidades y Números

We use Ser when we speak about amounts and numbers in Spanish. We use Ser to say an amount or number in math, whether it is the sum, the difference, the square of, the cube of, etc. We use Ser when we generally speak of amounts, whether its a collective group, a total, a weight, or any other measure.

Check out these examples:

¿Cuánto **es**? **Son** tres libras.
How much **is** it? It**'s** three pounds.

¿Pero cuánto **es** suficiente?
But how much **is** enough?

¿Cuánto **es** tres mas dos? **Son** cinco.
How much **is** three plus two? It **is** five.

Tres por ocho **son** veinticuatro.
Three times eight **is** twenty-four.

La raíz cúbica de 64 **es** 4.
The cube root of 64 **is** 4.

Side Note: Notice that if the number is plural, sometimes we can use **son** in Spanish, whereas in English, we still use **is**.

We use **es igual a** to say things are equal to something else:

b=a x c significa: b **es** igual a a por c.
b=a x c means: a **is** equal to a times c.

We use Ser for generally numbering things or people:

Mi hermano y yo **somos** dos personas distintas.
My brother and I **are** two different people.

Fueron tres cachorros que salieron del patio trasero.
It **was** three puppies that got out of the backyard.

 Exercise 21.

1. Esta cantidad de harina _____ suficiente para hacer una torta.
This amount of flour is enough to make a cake.

2. Doce dividido entre tres _____ cuatro.
Twelve divided by three is four.

3. El cuadrado de un número x _____ "x al cuadrado." Se escribe como "x2."
The square of a number x is "x squared." It is written as "x2."

4. Ellos _____ dos personas distintas.
They are two different people.

5. Tres libras mas una libra _____ igual a cuatro libras.
Three pounds plus one pound is equal to four pounds.

Predicate Nominatives—El Predicado Nominal

A predicate nominative, also know as a predicate noun, is when we say that *something IS something*. We use a linking verb to connect the two nouns. There are several linking verbs that we use in English, such as taste, smell, sound, feel, seem, turn into, etc. For example:

This **tastes** good.
That **smells** bad.
The song **sounds** great.
The fur **feels** soft.
Medical textbooks **seem** difficult.
Sugar **turns into** alcohol when combined with fermented fruit and yeast.

In this section, of course, we will use the linking verb "to be". In Spanish, we use Ser. You will realize that the lines may feel a little blurred, in that some of these example sentences fit into other categories as well. But don't worry, language is full of blurry lines. The more we practice, read, write, and listen to Spanish, the lines will darken, believe it or not.

An easy way of remembering what we mean by a *predicate nominative* is by thinking:

*This **equals** that.*

Ella **es** escritora.
She **is** a writer.

In the above sentence, **Ella** is the *subject*. **Writer** is the *predicate noun*.

Ella **es** una buena madre para sus hijos.
She **is** a good mother to her children.

In the above sentence, **Ella** is the *subject*. **Madre** is the *predicate noun*.

We can even compound the predicate noun, like this:

Jacobo **es** un buen *profesor, padre, y amigo.*
Jacobo **is** a good *teacher, father, and friend.*

 Side Note: We can use Estar in a similar fashion when talking about **conditions**, in which we use adverbs. For example:

El herido **está** mejor.
The injury **is** better.

(The adverb, and the condition, is "mejor/better".)

Side Note: We will cover more on conditions soon in the section called *"Conditions"*.

Exercise 22.

1. Carlos _____ un buen oficial. Trabaja muy duro.
Carlos is a good officer. He works very hard.

2. Los carros japoneses _____ vehículos muy populares aquí en los Estados Unidos.
Japanese cars are very popular vehicles here in the United

States.

3. Juan 1:1-2 dice "En el principio era el Verbo y el Verbo
_____ con Dios, y el Verbo _____ Dios."
John 1:1-2 says "In the beginning was the Word and the
Word was with God, and the Word was God."

4. El juguete favorito de Shawna _____ su erizo que
chilla cuando se aprieta.
Shawna's favorite toy is her hedgehog that squeaks when
you squeeze it.

5. La comida favorita de nuestros hijos debe _____ la
pizza.
Our kids' favorite food must be pizza.

Commands (The Imperative)—Los Mandatos (El Imperativo)

Now we'll dive into the use of the imperative form of Ser. This, simply put, is when we use Ser to give commands, orders, or demands to someone else, or something else, whenever we want to say "Be!" or "Don't be!"

For example:

Be a good person your whole life.
Be smart in all you do and things will go well.
Always **be** nice to your sister. You hear me?
Don't **be** stupid!

The imperative form, or command form, of the Spanish verb Ser is as follows. (This list is also in the back of the book for quick reference later on.)

Afirmative— "be"

(tú)	sé
(usted)	sea
(nosotros)	seamos (In English we say "Let's be.")
(vosotros)	sed
(ustedes)	sean

Negative— "don't be"

(tú)	no seas
(usted)	no sea
(nosotros)	no seamos
(vosotros)	no seáis
(ustedes)	no sean

This is what it looks like:

73

Sé una buena persona toda tu vida
Be a good person your whole life.

¡No **seas** estúpido!
Don't **be** stupid!

Sea usted una buena persona toda su vida.
Be a good person your whole life.

Seamos buenas personas todas nuestras vidas.
Let's be good people our whole lives.

No **seamos** malas personas.
Let's not **be** bad people.

Sé listo en todo lo que hagas, y todo te va a ir bien.
Be smart in all you do and everything will go well for you.

Sea usted listo en todo lo que haga, y todo le va a ir bien.
Be smart in all you do and everything will go well for you.

Vosotros siempre **sed** amables con vuestra hermana. ¿Me oís?

You guys always **be** nice to your sister. You hear me?

Ustedes siempre **sean** amables con su hermana. ¿Me oyen?

You guys always **be** nice to your sister. You hear me?

Ustedes ya no **sean** malos con ella.
Don't **be** mean to her anymore.

Sé listo: ¡protégete!
Be smart: protect yourself!

Exercise 23.

1. Vosotros _____ inteligentes.
Be smart.

2. No _____ aburrido, profesor. Díganos algo
gracioso. (usted)
Don't be boring, teacher. Tell us something funny.

3.Haz algo bueno. _____ presidente cuando seas
grande. (tú)
Do something good. Be president when you grow up.

4. ! _____ buenos! (ustedes)
You all be good!

5. No _____ malagradecidos con vuestra abuela.
(vosotros)
Do not be ungrateful to your grandmother.

CHAPTER FOUR

Uses of Estar

Uses of Estar—Usos de Estar

Now we'll get into the many uses of the verb **Estar**. As mentioned previously, it is commonly and accurately taught that **Ser** is the *essence* of something and **Estar** is the *condition* of something. Estar is used when talking about how something is at a specific point in time. If you can ask, "What is the condition of something or someone?" or "Where is it?", you can use Estar. For example:

¿Dónde **estás** en este momento?
Where **are** you right now?

¿Y cómo **estás** en este momento?
And how **are** you right now?

Side Note: **Estar** is derived from the Latin word *stare*, which means "stand", and is where we get the English word *state*. Therefore, Estar is used to describe the *state* of things, and to tell us where they *stand*.

We'll be covering lots of information concerning the uses of Estar. Some of the uses of Estar that we'll cover in this section are the following, to name a few:

- Greetings
- Location and Position (but not Events)
- Present Progressive
- Conditions
- Civil Status
- Results of an Action
- Commands
- Expressions

Greetings—Saludos

Throughout our daily lives we often greet people— whether in person, on the phone, via email, text messaging, and so on. In every language, there are various ways to greet others. We use phrases such as "Hello"; "How are you?"; "Good morning", "Good day", etc. In this section, we will concentrate on the greetings that use Estar. …I know. Shocker, right?

¿Cómo **estás**? (tú)
¿Cómo **está** usted?
¿Cómo **están** ustedes?
¿Cómo **estáis**? (vosotros)
How **are** you?

¿Cómo has **estado**? (tú)
¿Cómo ha **estado** usted?
¿Cómo han **estado** ustedes?
¿Cómo habéis **estado**? (vosotros)
How have you **been**?

¿Cómo **está** la familia?
How**'s** the family?

Mi hijo menor ha **estado** enfermo.
My youngest son has **been** sick.

Buen día. ¿**Estás** bien?
Good day. **Are** you doing well?

Estoy bien, gracias. ¿Y tú?
I**'m** fine, thanks. And you?

Exercise 24.

1. ¡Yo _____ estupendamente!
I'm doing great!

2. (Por teléfono) Bueno. ¿Quién habla? ¡Pedro! ¿Cómo has _____?
(On the phone) Hello. Who is it? Pedro! How have you been?

3. Y tu hermana mayor, ¿Cómo _____ ella?
What about your older sister, how is she?

4. Estamos bien. Y ustedes, ¿Cómo _____?
We're well. (or more commonly: We're good.) And you (all/guys), how are you?

5. He pasado muchas noches sin dormir, pero _____ bien.
I have had many sleepless nights, but I'm fine.

Location and Position (But Not Events)— Ubicación y Posición (Pero Eventos, No)

When speaking of locations, we always use Estar, except when talking about where an event is taking place or being held. *"La fiesta es allí."* Simply put, we use Estar to express where something is located, and how far or close something or someone is.

Side Note: We covered events in the section *"Location of Events"*.

Los jugadores **están** en el estadio, donde va a ser el partido.
The players **are** in the stadium, where the game will be held.

El Gran Cañón **está** en el estado de Arizona.
The Grand Canyon **is** in the state of Arizona.

La ciudad de Seúl **está** en Corea del Sur.
The city of Seoul **is** in South Korea.

La ciudad de México D.F. **está** a 2,161.4 kilómetros de Tucson, Arizona.
Mexico City **is** 2,161.4 kilometers from Tucson, Arizona.

La ciudad de Lima **está** en Perú. Es la capital de aquel país.
The city of Lima **is** in Peru. It is the capital of that country.

El cortauñas **está** sobre el escritorio.
The nail clippers **are** on top of the desk.

El ratón **está** dentro de la caja.
The mouse **is** inside the box.

80

Exercise 25.

1. ¿Dónde _____ mis guantes?
Where are my gloves?

2. Aunque tú _____ allí, no importa, porque no te dejan entrar.
Even though you are there, it doesn't matter because they don't let you in.

3. La luna _____ muy lejos de la tierra.
The moon is very far from the earth.

4. El partido _____ en el parque donde vimos toda la comida.
The game was in the park where we saw all the food.

5. Siempre que mi tía Beca _____ con nuestra familia, mi tío Adán tiende a enfadarse.
Whenever my aunt Beca is with our family, my uncle Adán tends to get angry.

Present Progressive—El Presente Progresivo

The present progressive **in English** is a verb form that uses a conjugation of "to be" followed by a word ending in **-ing** (called a present participle). It is used to express that an action is currently in progress, or is being repeated.

I **am** eat**ing**.
We **are** danc**ing**.
The lady in the drawing **is** runn**ing**.
You **are** read**ing**.

Side Note: In Spanish, we call the participle *"el gerundio"*, not to be confused with the English word *gerund*, which is a verb used as a noun.

In Spanish, we use a form of Ser, followed by a word ending in **-ando** or **-iendo** depending on whether the verb is an **-ar**, **-er**, or **-ir** verb.

Caminar = Alberto **está caminando**.
To walk = Alberto **is walking**.

Fallecer = El anciano **está falleciendo**.
To pass away = The old man **is passing away**.

Escupir = Flor **está escupiendo**.
To spit = Flor **is spitting**.

Estudiar = Las chicas **están estudiando**.
To study = The girls **are studying**.

Side Note: In English, we use the progressive tense to explain what is happening *at the moment, is in progress, or is repeating itself.* …And in English, we commonly use the present progressive to say that something will happen in the future, as in this sentence:

Juliana **is cooking** chicken and rice tomorrow night. (This will happen in the future.)

In Spanish, this is **NOT** the case. We only use the progressive tense to describe what's going on right now, right this second, right this moment, right at a specific moment in time, with an action that is progressive, or with an action that is being repeated.

In Spanish, we say the same sentence like this:

Juliana **va a cocinar** pollo con arroz mañana por la noche.
Juliana **is going to cook** chicken with rice tomorrow night.

Or…

Juliana **cocinará** pollo con arroz mañana por la noche.
Juliana **will cook** chicken and rice tomorrow night.

If we are expressing that Juliana is cooking *right now*, we say:

Juliana **está cocinando** pollo con arroz (en este momento).
Juliana **is cooking** chicken and rice (right now).

Exercise 26.

1. Yo _____ ahora mismo.
I am studying right now.

2. Si te _____, hay que irte ya.
If you are getting angry, you need to leave now.

3. Noemí _____ pantalones azules hoy.
Noemí is wearing blue pants today.

4. Raquel _____ al lado del niño para que aprenda.
Raquel is painting alongside the boy so that he can learn.

5. Más vale que te _____ para salir. Vamos a llegar
tarde.
You'd better be getting ready to leave. We're going to be
late.

Conditions Of Things—Las Condiciones

Estar is used when we are speaking of the condition that someone or something is in at the moment.

For example, we use Estar to express a temporary state that someone is in, such as:

A temporary physical state of people.

Estoy *enfermo* hoy. No voy al trabajo.
I **am** *sick* today. I'm not going to work.

Por la madrugada, **estoy** muy *cansado*. Pero por la tarde, **estoy** muy *despierto* y *lleno* de energía, y lleno de ganas de participar.
At dawn I **am** very *tired*. But in the afternoon, I **am** *awake* and *full of energy*, and *ready for action*.

A temporary physical state of something.

¿*Cómo* **está** la carne? La carne **está** *salada*.
How is the meat. The meat **is** *salty*. (…because it's not always salty, it's not its nature.)

A temporary mental state.

Los polítocos **estaban** muy *confundidos* al oír las noticias.
The politicians **were** very *confused* when they heard the news. (They are not always confused.)

Luís **está** un poco *loco* esta tarde. No sé por qué.
Luís **is** a little *crazy* this evening. I don't know why. (He's not usually crazy, but this evening he is.)

A temporary emotion or feeling.

Estoy muy *enojado* contigo.
I **am** very *mad* at you. (I'm not usually mad, but I'm mad right now. That's my condition at the moment and it will go away eventually.)

Mi esposa y yo **estamos** *preocupados* por lo ocurrido.
My wife and I **are** *worried* because of what happened. (We're not usually worried, we're just worried right now because something unpleasant has happened.)

 Exercise 27.

1. Marta _____ triste después del funeral. Ahora _____ mejor.
Marta was sad after the funeral. Now she is better.

2. A Samuel le dio cuenta de que su perro _____ enfermo.
Samuel realized that his dog was sick.

3. Ella _____ contenta porque su hija le trajo un dibujo que hizo en la escuela.
She is happy because her daughter brought her a drawing that she made in school.

4. Eliezer _____ bien vestido esta noche, ¿no?
Eliezer is well dressed tonight, isn't he?

5. La novia de Rogelio, Lisa, _____ celosa ayer porque Amanda, quien es muy bella, vino a visitarlo y se quedó en su casa durante dos horas.
Rogelio's girlfriend, Lisa, was jealous yesterday because Amanda, who is very beautiful, came to visit him and she stayed at his house for two hours.

Civil Status—El Estado Civil

Civil status refers to whether someone is:

Soltero— Single
Prometido— Engaged
Casado— Married
Separado— Separated (or Estranged)
Divorciado— Divorced
Viudo— Widowed
Adoptado— Adopted
Muerto— Dead
Vivo— Alive
Desaparecido— Missing

When learning about how to talk about civil status, many Spanish learners find this confusing. Why would we use Estar? Some of these words seem so permanent and for sure would require the use of Ser.

Here's a good rule of thumb:

Civil status is a **state of being**. Someone can be in a state of marriage, a state of death, a state of separation, and so on. Hence they are in a *state of being*. You can remember that we use Estar to express civil status in Spanish by remembering the following:

Civil Status— Estado Civil.

State = Estado

The word "Estado" comes from the word "Estar".

Here are some examples:

¿Cuál es tu estado civil?

What is your marital status?

¿**Estás** casado, Jorge? No, **estoy** soltero.
Are you married, Jorge? No, I **am** single. (This is Jorge's situation at the moment, but it could change if he's lucky, right? So here we can use Estar.

¿**Estás** soltero? Sí, **estoy** soltero.
Are you single? Yes, I **am** single.

Yo no. **Estoy** divorciado.
Not me. I **am** divorced.

Side Note: If someone is filling out a form or application of some type, he or she may see that the question is:

¿**Es** usted soltero? (Is *single* your civil status?)

Instead of:

¿**Está** usted soltero? (Is this your situation at the moment, which can change?)

We can choose one verb or the other for **emphasis**. *Estar can be used to* **emphasize** *that something is temporal or habitual, while Ser would be used to* **emphasize** *civil status.*

Here are some more examples of talking about one's civil state:

Cuando Sergio **estaba** vivo, ganaba mucho dinero. Pero ya no, ya que **está** muerto.
When Sergio **was** alive, he earned a lot of money. But not anymore, since he **is** dead.

That being said, we still use Ser when speaking of a person's normality. For example, when we use "un/una" in this way:

Tomás **es** *un* hombre soltero. **Está** soltero.
Tomás **is** a single man. He **is** single.

Ana **es** *una* mujer viuda. **Está** viuda.
Ana **is** a widowed women. She **is** widowed.

Y yo **soy** *una* persona divorciada. **Estoy** divorciado.
And I **am** a divorced person. I **am** divorced.

So, you can see that in the above sentences that first, we are expressing **what the person is**, then we describe the **state that that person is in**.

 **Side Note:** Using the word viuda/viudo can be confusing, but with practice, it becomes simple:

Luz **es** una viuda.
Luz **is** a widow.

But if we say that Luz's husband died, the result of that action is:

Luz **está** viuda.
Luz **is** widowed.

We'll be looking more into results of actions in the section called, you guessed it, *"Results of an Action"*.

Important to Know

We usually use Estar with civil status because we are **emphasizing the state of someone**. However, it is very important to know that Ser is also used to talk about civil status, although not near as common as using Estar. It is also important to know that this does **not** mean that the two verbs are exactly interchangeable with civil status adjectives, or any other qualifying adjective, since using one verb or the other **will** change the meaning, even if sometimes only slightly.

For example, if you **feel** that the civil situation you are talking about (married, single, widowed) at the moment is part of a class (single people, married people, widowers) you can choose to use Ser; but if you **feel** the situation is just a **state** in the moment which you are talking about, you can choose Estar.

Depending on what meaning we intend to express, we may choose either Ser or Estar for civil Status.

To expound further, above we saw the sentence:

*Luz **es** una viuda.*

Here, **viuda** is a noun, and when we use the formula

Somebody + is + a something

…it **automatically** means that we are going to use **Ser**.

So if we are expressing **what someone is**, we use Ser if we use a noun, as shown above. And if we say that **someone is something**, and that something is a qualifying adjective, in this case, a civil status adjective, we have the *choice* of using Ser.

*Luz **es** viuda.*

Here, we are talking about what Luz **is,** as opposed to what state she is in. She **is something**. Even though **viuda** here is an adjective, we are expressing **what** Luz is, and **viuda** is acting as a noun here. Here are some more examples:

What is *Luz?*

Luz **es** una mujer viuda.
Luz **is** a widowed woman.

Luz **es** viuda.
Luz **is** a widow.

How is *Luz since her husband passed away?*

Ahora, Luz **está** viuda.

What is *Salvador?*

Salvador **es** un hombre soltero.
Salvador **is** a single man.

Salvador **es** soltero.
Salvador **is** single.

How is *Salvador, now that he broke up with his girlfriend?*
(What state is he in now?)

Salvador **está** soltero, ya que rompió con su novia.
Salvador **is** single since he broke up with his girlfriend.

 Exercise 28.

1. Carlos y Lupe _____ casados.
Carlos and Lupe are married.

2. Felipe ya no _____ un hombre soltero, porque

ahora se casó. _____ casado.

    Felipe is no longer a single man because he got married. He is married.

    3. El marido de Luz falleció el año pasado. Luz _____ viuda.

    Luz's husband passed away last year. Luz is widowed.

    4. Un hombre que _____ soltero no _____ casado.

    A man who is single is not married.

    5. Hay que hacer todo lo que podamos mientras _____ vivos.

    We have to do all we can while we are alive.

Results Of An Action—Los Resultados De Una Acción

Many verbs express action, for example: standing, sitting, lying down, etc. To express the *result* of an action, we use Estar, followed by a past participle.

Example:

Sentarse— to sit down

What action did I take?
Me senté en la silla.
I sat on the chair.

What state am I in now? What's the result?
Estoy sentado en la silla.
I **am** seated (sitting) on the chair.

"**Estoy** sentado" is the result of "Me senté".

Here's another one:

Acostarse— to lie down

What action did he take?
Se acostó en la cama.
He lay down on the bed.

What state is he in now? What's the result?
Está acostado en la cama.
He is lying down on the bed.

And yet another example:

Abrir algo— to open something

What action did the cook take?

93

El cocinero abrió la lata.
The cook opened the can.

What state is the can in now? What's the result?
La lata **está** abierta.
The can **is** open.

One more for good measure:

Escribir— to write

What action did Linda take?
Linda escribió una carta.
Linda wrote a letter.

What state is the letter in now? What's the result?
Una carta está escrita.
A letter is written.

We can also express results of action using the past tense. In the following sentence, we speak of the state of the book *now*. The book was written at that time.

El libro ya **estaba** escrito para el viernes.
The book **was** already written by Friday.

If the subject of the sentence is also the object, in other words, if the subject received that action on itself, we can use **Ser**.

Juanito escribió el libro.
Juanito wrote the book.

(Subject *Juanito* acting on the object *book*.)

So then…

El libro **fue escrito** por Juanito.
The book **was written** by Juanito.

(The object *book* is receiving the action, by Juanito. *By* is a preposition, so *Juanito* in this sentence is not the subject, the *book*

94

is.)

Here's a comparison of a building that is **already torn down** and a building **being torn down**, receiving the action:

Cuando pasé por esa calle, vi que el edificio **estaba** derribado.
When I passed through that street, I saw that the building **was** torn down.

(The building was already in a **state** of having been torn down.)

But:

Antes de que yo pasara por esa calle, el edificio **fue** derribado (por alguien).
Before I passed through that street, the building **was** torn down (by somebody).

(Here, the emphasis is on the fact that the building had been torn down **by somebody**.)

 Exercise 29.

1. El profesor se enojó. Él _____ enojado ahora.
The teacher got mad. He is angry now.

2. Los estudiantes se levantaron del piso. Ahora ellos _____ de pie.
The students got up from the floor. Now they are standing.

3. El gato se estiró en el sofá. El gato _____ estirado en el sofá.

The cat stretched out on the couch. The cat is stretched out on the couch.

4. Paré el coche al ver el perro. El coche _____ parado.

I stopped the car when I saw the dog. The car was stopped.

5. El autor escribió un libro de gramática española. El libro _____ escrito. El libro _____ escrito por el autor.

The author wrote a book on Spanish grammar. The book was written. The book was written by the author.

Commands (The Imperative)—Los Mandatos (El Imperativo)

Now we'll dive into the use of the imperative form of Estar. We can use Estar to give commands, orders, or demands to someone else, or something else, whenever we want to say "Be!" or "Don't be!"

The imperative form, or command form, of the Spanish verb Estar is as follows:

Affirmative— "be"

(tú)	está
(Ud.)	esté
(nosotros)	estemos (let's be)
(vosotros)	estad
(Uds.)	estén

Negative— "don't be"

(tú)	no estés
(usted)	no esté
(nosotros)	no estemos
(vosotros)	no estéis
(ustedes)	no estén

For example:

¡**Está** quieto, niño!
Be still, kid!

Mi abuela me gritó, "¡**Está** tú aquí a las tres de la tarde!"
My grandmother yelled out to me, "**Be** here at three in the afternoon."

No **estén** tristes, mis hijos.
Don't **be** sad, my children.

Pretty straight forward, right? Easy peasy.

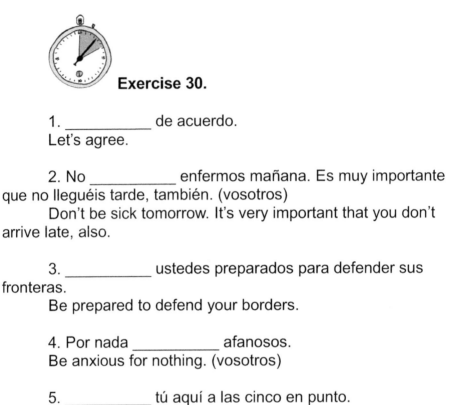 **Exercise 30.**

1. _____ de acuerdo.
Let's agree.

2. No _____ enfermos mañana. Es muy importante que no lleguéis tarde, también. (vosotros)
Don't be sick tomorrow. It's very important that you don't arrive late, also.

3. _____ ustedes preparados para defender sus fronteras.
Be prepared to defend your borders.

4. Por nada _____ afanosos.
Be anxious for nothing. (vosotros)

5. _____ tú aquí a las cinco en punto.
Be here at five o'clock.

Expressions With Estar—Expresiones Que Usan Estar

Estar is used with a great myriad of expressions in Spanish — and using them in your speech will help you to become more fluent. What's more, becoming familiar with these expressions will help you better ingrain in your mind the uses of Estar. It's a "win-win" situation!

Estar por signifies being in the mood for something.

Mi perra, Shawna, está por tomar café. Es muy rara.
My dog, Shawna, is in the mood to drink coffee. She is very strange.

Estar para signifies something that is about to happen in the near future.

El autobús está para salir.
The bus is about to leave./The bus will leave soon.

Side Note: Entire books have been written on Por and Para, and the best one I have found is the the very in-depth book written by Gordon and Cynthia Smith-Durán called *Pocket Por and Para.*

SPANISH EXPRESSIONS USING ESTAR

Estar de acuerdo— *to be in agreement*

Los socios están de acuerdo.
The associates are in agreement.

Estar conforme con— *to be in agreement with*

99

Jimena está conforme con el trato.
Jimena is in agreement with the deal.

Estar en las nubes— to daydream

Miguel, que estaba sentado en el asiento trasero, estaba en
las nubes durante la clase.
Miguel, who was sitting in the seat in the back, was
daydreaming during the class.

Estar en camino— to be on the way

Estaba en camino al trabajo cuando vi la vaca en la calle.
I was on the way to work when I saw the cow in the road.

Estar de pie— to be standing

Los ancianos están sentados. Los jóvenes están de pie.
The elderly folks are sitting down. The youngsters are
standing.

Está despejado— it's clear

El cielo está despejado ahora.
The sky is now clear.

Estar de mal humor— to be in a bad mood

No quiero hablar con él porque siempre está de mal humor.
I don't want to speak to him because he is always in a bad
mood.

Estar de más— unnecessary, too much

Ella le está exigiendo veinte dólares pero eso está de más.
She is demanding twenty dollars from him, but that is too
much.

Estar fuera de sí— to be beside oneself emotionally

Elizabeth estaba tan fuera de sí que rompió todo lo que encontraba en su camino.
Elizabeth was so beside herself that she broke everything that was in her way.

Estar de sobra— to be in excess

Los melocotones que compraron están de sobra.
The peaches they bought are in excess.

Estar loco de remate— to be completely crazy

Agustín está loco de remate.
Agustín is completely crazy.

Estar en condiciones— to be in good shape

El restaurante finalmente está en condiciones para recibir muchos clientes.
The restaurant is finally in good enough shape to receive many customers.

Estar en forma— to be in good shape

Camila es muy bella y está en forma.
Camila is very beautiful and she is in good shape.

Estar pez— to ignore (something), to know nothing about (something)

David está pez en Biología.
David knows nothing about Biology.

Estar sin blanca— to be flat broke

No podemos ir a comer porque estamos sin blanca.
We can't go eat because we are flat broke.

Estar en la luna— to have one's head in the clouds

Leonardo llegó tarde y por eso está en la luna.

Leonardo came late and that is why he has his head is in the clouds.

Estar de vuelta— to be back

El doctor estará de vuelta en una hora. Salió a comer.
The doctor will be back in one hour. He went to lunch.

Estar hecho polvo— to be worn out

Hiciste tanto ejercicio y ahora estás hecho polvo. Descansa ya.
You did so much exercise and now you are worn out. Just rest.

Estar hecho una fiera— to be furious

El jefe se fue y estaba hecho una fiera.
The boss left and he was furious.

Estar en un tris— to be about to happen

Que Susana se entere la verdad está en un tris.
Susana finding out the truth is about to happen.

Estar hecho una sopa— to be soaked

Después de la lluvia los cachorros estaban hechos una sopa.
After the rain the puppies were soaked.

Estar al corriente de— to be up to date

Los estudiantes necesitan estar al corriente de las noticias de su país.
The students need to be up to date with their country's news.

Estar a dos velas— to be broke

Mis tíos están a dos velas después de haber perdido sus trabajos.

My aunt and uncle are broke after having lost their jobs.

Estar como pez en el agua— *to be right at home*

Mi amiga que nos visitó hace dos meses estaba como pez en el agua aquí.
My friend that visited us two months ago was right at home here.

Estar de paso— *to be passing through*

No se moleste, solamente estoy de paso.
Don't bother, I am just passing through.

 Exercise 31.

1. _____ por comer algo.
I'm in the mood to eat something.

2. El momento que esperábamos _____ al caer.
The moment we were waiting for is about to occur.

3. Sara _____ de buen humor porque acaba de comprar un carro.
Sara is in a good mood because she just bought a car.

4. Emiliano _____ en el limbo después de escuchar la noticia.
Emiliano was feeling lost after hearing the news.

5. Catalina _____ a sus anchas en la casa de su novio.
Catalina was very comfortable in her boyfriend's house.

CHAPTER FIVE

Using Either Ser or Estar

Using Either Ser or Estar—Usar O Ser O Estar

So far, we have learned many uses of Ser and Estar. Although there is no *perfect* rule for their usage, we cannot just fall back on the misleading rule that Ser is permanent and Estar is temporary. The rule fits in many ways, but not always. It's not reliable. It's not foolproof. We have seen that the same sentence can use either Ser or Estar, and they both can sound correct. But we have to be careful with it, because whether we use Ser or Estar *can and will* change the meaning of the sentence in question. It can change what we *intend* to say, and if we do not use these fundamental verbs correctly, it can cause problems and confusion.

Now we will take a look into how Ser and Estar cross paths, interchange, blur the lines, and get all tangled up with each other… in attempt to understand just how they can impact the meaning of what we are saying.

The Intentions Of The Speaker—Las Intenciones Del Hablante

It is important to understand that the intentions of the speaker, in other words, what the speaker really wants to get across, will dictate the verb that he choses to use in order to accurately convey an idea.

Look at this sentence using Ser:

La chica **es** bella.
The girl **is** beautiful.

However, using Estar instead of Ser in the same sentence can alter the meaning:

Está bella hoy.
She *looks* beautiful today.

Let's give this sentence some context…

¿Ella es la chica que habíamos visto ayer? ¡**Está** bella hoy! ¿Podría ser la misma chica?
Is that the girl we had seen yesterday? She **is** beautiful today! Could it be the same girl?

What happened here? Well, the girl is beautiful. That's a personal trait of hers. She's always beautiful, so we use Ser. However, by using Estar, we convey the idea that today she appears more beautiful than she *normally* does. Maybe she got her hair done. Maybe it's her makeup or her new outfit. You see, she is now in a *state* of extraordinary beauty, even more than yesterday. Therefore, we can use Estar this time. In English, we usually just change the verb we are using. For example, here we changed *"is"* to *"looks"* to express this idea that now she is more beautiful than yesterday.

She **is** beautiful.

But she **looks** *really* beautiful today!

…Whereas in Spanish, we can simply denote this difference in our thinking by using Estar instead of Ser.

To make it clearer, we could think of it this way:

Gabriel is the father. Valentina is the cute daughter. She is always cute and pretty. Today she is getting ready for her first school dance and puts on the new clothes her dad bought her. She does her hair really nice and comes out of her room to show her dad. Gabriel takes one look at his daughter and proclaims:

¡Valentina! ¡Qué bonita **estás** esta tarde!
Valentina! How pretty you **are** this evening! (How pretty you **look** this evening.)

Now, Gabriel is not saying this because his daughter is usually an ugly little bugger. She has always been pretty. But this evening, she fixed herself up and looks amazing! Estar is used because of the current circumstances.

We see the same thing with other personal traits. For example, let's talk about Joaquín, a normally very happy guy…

Joaquín **es** una persona alegre.
Joaquín **is** a jolly person.

We can simplify this sentence to:

Joaquín es alegre.
Joaquín is jolly.

He's just a happy person in general. That's how he is. A happy guy. It's a personal trait of his.

But if we substitute Ser with Estar…

Joaquín **está** triste hoy porque murió su perro. Normalmente, él es una persona alegre.

Joaquín **is** sad today because his dog died. Normally, he is a joyful person.

Joaquín is normally a jolly, happy, joyful guy. We know this about him. However, his dog, whom he loved for many years, has just passed away. On this sad day, the joy is gone and it is replaced with mourning. Therefore, we can now accurately say that Joaquín is not his own, happy self. He is sad. But this is a temporary state for him, *a condition that will change with time*, so it would be unfit to use Ser in this case, and more appropriate to use Estar to describe his current condition.

Joaquín **está** triste hoy.

In conclusion, just exactly **which** verb we use, whether it be Ser or Estar, will depend on what exactly it is that we want to convey to our listener.

If we had chosen to say…

Joaquín **es** triste.

…then it would have meant that he is normally a sad guy, that he is sad all the time, and it is his personal essence. This is not the case for Joaquín.

Don't worry about Joaquín. He'll be alright later on down the line.

Normally Unchanging Conditions— Condiciones Que Normalmente No Cambian

We use Ser to talk about conditions that generally do not change. With Ser, we can describe just how something is, most of the time, generally, usually, or all the time. Here are some examples:

Tutendo, Colombia **es** muy lluviosa.
Tutendo, Colombia **is** very rainy.

Tutendo is a place where it rains all the time. It is very rainy there. It doesn't change, therefore, we use Ser.

Manzanas "Arkansas Black" **son** de color rojo oscuro.
"Arkansas Black" apples **are** dark red.

This type of apple is always dark red. We always expect it to be dark red, so we use Ser.

On the other hand, if the apple is rotten and has turned black, we use Estar because the apple is generally not black and rotten. It is a condition that has changed. The apple is now in a different state. We usually don't expect the apple to be rotten. We use Estar for this condition.

Esta manzana en la canasta está negra y podrida. Normalmente, este tipo de manzana es rojo.
This apple in the basket is black and rotten. Typically, this type of apple is red.

Crazy Jorge

Jorge was born crazy. He grew up crazy. He is just a crazy person. He is never *not* crazy. He is described as a crazy person by anyone who knows him. We will use Ser to describe this unchanging condition.

Jorge **es** una persona loca.
Jorge **is** a crazy person.

Or, in a shortened version:

Jorge **es** loco.
Jorge **is** crazy.

…which essentially is the same thing as "Jorge es una persona loca." Jorge is a crazy person. We can see that the two sentences mean the same thing, because they are describing what this guy is. …what his nature is…

Jorge **es** loco.

However, Pilar is generally a nice person. One day she came home from work and checked her mail. When she saw that her electric bill was far higher than normal this month, she went crazy. At least just for a moment.

Pilar **está** loca en este momento. Acaba de ver la factura de electricidad. Generalmente, Pilar **es** una persona muy contenta.

Pilar **is** crazy right now. She just saw the electric bill. Pilar **is** usually a very happy person.

But now, she is in a *state of craziness*.

Do you see the difference?

White Snow, Yellow Snow—Nieve Blanca, Nieve Amarilla

As we have discussed, people and things have traits, characteristics, and essence— something that they are, which we describe using Ser. But when a person or thing is in a new or different state or condition, we can use Estar.

Take the example of snow, which is white. When we think of snow, we picture it white. Why? Because it is its nature, its essence. It's just white. Right?

Side Note: Have you ever heard the phrase, "Don't eat the yellow snow?" Well, let's talk a bit about yellow snow...

Generalmente, la nieve **es** blanca. Sin embargo, desde que llegó tu cachorro, la nieve **está** amarilla por aquí.

Snow **is** white. However, since your puppy arrived, the snow **is** yellow around here.

Tall House, Short House—Casa Alta, Casa Baja

We can use the example of a house to understand the changing state of something that *normally* does not change.

Esta casa **es** alta. Tiene dos plantas.
This house **is** tall. It has two floors.

Quitaron la planta de arriba para volver a construirla mejor. Ahora la casa **está** baja.
They removed the second floor to rebuild it better. Now it **is** low.

Acaban de arreglar la casa. Ahora **está** alta de nuevo.
They just finished fixing the house. Now it **is** tall again.

But generally, when things don't change, we say:

La casa **es** alta.
The house **is** tall. (The size of the house normally won't

change.)

Frozen Ice Cream, Melted Ice Cream— Helado Congelado, Helado Derretido

Why is ice cream called "ice cream"? Because it is a frozen, creamy, delicious treat. It's cold. Cold is its essence. When we think of ice cream, we picture it cold, right? Therefore, we use Ser to describe it.

¿Cómo **es** el helado? El helado **es** frío. Así **es**.
What **is** the ice cream **like**? Ice cream **is** cold. That's how it **is**.

Again, ice cream is cold and frozen and delicious. But its *state* can change. When we speak of something's state, we use Estar. Let's take a look at how ice cream's state can change.

El helado se ha derretido después de quedarse en la mesa todo el santo día. Ahora **está** derritido y tibio.
The ice cream has melted after being left on the table the whole friggin' day. Now it **is** melted and lukewarm.

When Both Can Be Used—Cuando Los Dos Se Pueden Usar

When we want to ask "How much is it?" when referring to a price that has changed from its usual value, we can use Estar.

¿Y estos calcetines en esta caja? ¿A cuánto **están** ahora? Ayer **estaban** a diez dólares el paquete.
What about these socks in this box? How much **are** they right now? Yesterday they **were** ten dollars a pack.

Side Note: We will discuss prices further in the upcoming section, "Prices Using Both Ser and Estar".

Ser/Estar Can Change The Meaning— Ser/Estar Pueden Cambiar El Sentido

Whether we choose to use Ser or we choose to use Estar, it can make an impact on the rest of the sentence by effecting the relationship between what is *doing* the action and what is *receiving* the action. Using Ser can make a sentence mean one thing, while using Estar can give the sentence an entirely different meaning.

Here is a list of some words that can change their meaning depending on which "to be" verb they follow.

Ser aburrido— to be boring
Estar aburrido— to be bored

La clase de matemáticas **es** muy **aburrida**. **Estoy aburrido** cuando estoy en esa clase.
The math class **is** very **boring**. I **am bored** when I am in that class.

Ser cansado— to be tiring
Estar cansado— to be tired

Ser bombero **es cansado**. Trabajé esta mañana en la estación de bomberos. **Estoy cansado** ya.
Being a fireman **is tiring**. I worked this morning at the fire station. I **am tired** now.

Ser grave— to be serious (a situation)
Estar grave— to be seriously ill

El accidente **fue** muy **grave**. El conductor estaba vomitando cuando chocó el auto. Está en el hospital porque **está** muy **grave** y tiene las piernas rotas.
The accident **was** very **serious**. The driver was vomiting when he crashed the car. He is in the hospital because he **is seriously ill** and has broken legs.

Ser listo— to be clever, sharp, smart
Estar listo— to be ready, prepared

Daniel **es** un estudiante muy **listo**. Ha estudiado mucho y creo que **está listo** para el examen.
Daniel **is** a very **sharp** student. He has studied a lot and I believe he **is ready** for the test.

Ser malo— to be bad
Estar malo— to be sick, ill

El niño, Alonso, **es malo**. Pegó a su hermano menor aunque **estaba malo**.
The little boy, Alonso, **is bad**. He hit his little brother even though he **was sick**.

Ser orgulloso— to be conceited
Estar orgulloso— to be proud

Anita no **es orgullosa** en absoluto. Sus papás **están** muy **orgullosos** de los esfuerzos de Anita que ha hecho para ayudar a otros.
Anita is not conceited at all. Her parents are very proud of her efforts to help others.

Ser moreno— to be dark-skinned, dark-complected
Estar moreno— to be tan, dark (in a state of being tanned-skinned)

Armando ya **era moreno**, pero su novia, Felipa, **está morena** porque acaba de pasar tres días en la playa.
Armando **was** already **dark-complected**, but his girlfriend, Felipa, **is dark** because she has just spent three days on the beach.

Ser pálido— to be pale skinned
Estar pálido— to look pale (at the moment)

Cristóbal ya **era pálido**, pero su novia, Francesca, **está pálida** solamente porque se acaba de asustar.
Cristóbal was already pale, but his girlfriend, Francesca, is

pale only because she has just gotten scared.

Ser rico— to be rich
Estar rico— to be tasty or delicious (food), to be rich at the moment

Luciana **es rica**. Ella ha estado en el restaurante "Masa" en Nueva York. Se dice que la comida **está** muy **rica** allí. Obviamente, es muy caro comer allí también.
Luciana **is rich**. She has been to the restaurant "Masa" in New York City. They say that the food **is** very **tasty** there. Obviously, it is very expensive to eat there, too.

Ser seguro— to be safe, secure
Estar seguro— to be certain, sure

Creen que esto también significa que el avión **es seguro**. **Estoy seguro** de que muy pronto dispondremos de información más precisa.
They believe that this also means that this airplane **is safe**. I **am sure** that very soon we will have more accurate information.

Ser verde— to be green
Estar verde— to be unripe (fruit)

Ese plátano **es amarillo** como debería ser. Pero este plátano todavía **está verde**. Tendremos que esperar unos dos días más para poder comerlo cuando **esté amarillo**.
That banana **is yellow** as it should be. But this banana **is** still **green**. We will have to wait about two more days to be able to eat it when it **is yellow**.

Side Note: Did you notice that in the above sentences, we said that the "plátano *es* amarillo" but then later we said *"esté* amarillo"? *(Esté is the subjunctive form of está.)* That's because we were talking about the condition of the banana changing from green to yellow. To make it clearer, we usually think of a banana as being yellow, right? But when we talk about the banana changing color, in other words, changing it's state or condition, we use Estar. That's the cool thing about Spanish— we can express ourselves in more detail by the words that we choose to utilize! …Okay, let's continue…

Ser viejo— to be old
Estar viejo— to look old

Aquel coche **es viejo** y de baja calidad. No obstante, el coche de al lado no **está** tan **viejo**, ¿no?
That car over there **is old** and low quality. Nevertheless, the car next to it doesn't **look** so **old**, does it?

Ser joven— to be young
Estar joven— to look young

Yo siempre he creído que **ser joven** es difícil pero **estar joven** es fácil.
I have always believed that **being young** is difficult but **looking young** is easy.

Ser bueno— to be good
Estar bueno— to be fine, to be tasty (food), to be attractive (person)

Violeta **es** muy **buena** pero no **es** muy **bonita**. Pero Jasmín **está buena**. ¡Mírala!
Violeta is a very good person but she is not very pretty. But Jasmín **is attractive.** Look at her!

Ser vivo— to be sharp (person), quick
Estar vivo— to be alive

"La Palabra de Dios, entonces, **es viva** y eficaz en nuestra propia experiencia personal..." *Charles Spurgeon.* — Por eso creo que **estar vivo** es una bendición.
"The Word of God, then, **is quick** and powerful in our own personal experience..." *Charles Spurgeon,* — That's why I believe that **being alive** is a blessing.

Ser abierto— to be open, sociable

Estar abierto— to be open (a door, a window)

El jefe **es** muy **abierto**, y siempre **está abiert**a la puerta de su oficina si quieres hablar con él.

The boss **is** very **sociable**, and his office door **is** always **open** if you want to talk to him.

Ser nervioso— to be a nervous person (as a personal trait)
Estar nervioso— to be nervous (in a state of nervousness at the time)

— ¿**Estás nerviosa**? Yo sí.
— Pues sí, porque tú **eres nerviosa, normalmente**. Tú **eres** una persona **nerviosa**.

"**Are** you **nervous**? I am."
"Of course **you are**, because you **are normally nervous**. You **are** a **nervous** person."

¿Cómo **eres** tú?
What **are** you like?

Estoy delgado y alto.
I **am** thin and tall.

¿Cómo **estás** tú?
How **are** you?

Estoy estupendamente.
I **am** doing great.

Prices Using Both Ser and Estar—Los Precios Con Ser y Estar

Throughout our lives, we talk a lot about how much something costs, or what its value is.

How much does it cost?

What is its value?

How much is it worth?

Or simply:

How much is it?

We even use phrases such as:

How much is it going for?

Well, we have the same kind of stuff in Spanish.

¿Cuánto cuesta?
How much does it cost?

¿Cuánto vale?
How much does it cost?
How much is it worth?

We can also use **Ser** for asking about prices and value.

*¿Cuánto **es**?*
*How much **is** it?*

In addition, we can use Estar for asking about prices as well, but in a different way. We can improve our Spanish fluency by saying it this way:

¿A cuánto **está**?
How much **is** it **going for**?

¿A cómo **está**?
How much **is** it **going for**?

You may hear these phrases in a market or produce store where prices may change regularly:

¿A cuánto está el kilo de carne de res molida hoy?
How much is a kilo of ground beef today?

Está a $1.99 el kilo.
It **is** $1.99 a kilo.

¿A cómo está la docena de huevos?
How much **is** a dozen eggs **going for**?

We can also use Estar in these phrases when we are talking about the value of currency:

¿A cuánto **está**?
How much **is** it (worth)?

¿A cuánto está el dólar en México hoy?
How much is the dollar **worth** in Mexico today?

¿A cómo está el euro en Argentina?
How much is the euro in Argentina?

EJERCICIOS

Using Either Ser or Estar—Usar o Ser o Estar

 Exercise 32.

1. La novia de Lucas _____ fea cuando lleva ese abrigo de piel.
Lucas' girlfriend looks ugly when she wears that fur coat.

2. Esta sopa coreana _____ una sopa fría, porque así se come en Corea del Sur.
This Korean soup is a cold soup because that's how it is eaten in South Korea.

3. Esta es una sopa fría, pero la mesera me la trajo caliente. ¿Por qué _____ caliente la sopa esta vez?
This is a cold soup, but the waitress brought it to me hot. Why is this soup hot this time?

4. Compré esta camisa de lana ayer y _____ grande. La eché a la secadora y mira lo que pasó. Ahora _____ pequeña.
I bought this wool shirt yesterday and it was big. I threw it in the dryer and look what happened. Now it's small.

5. Marina _____ una mujer encantadora y cariñosa, pero cuando fuimos a la tienda anoche, _____ muy enojada.
Marina is a pleasant and affectionate woman, but when we went to the store last night, she was very angry.

6. ¿Y ella, cómo es? Ella _____ bien callada. Siempre ha sido así.
And what is she like? She is really quiet. She's always been

like that.

7. Estuve en este dormitorio la semana pasada. Las paredes _____ verdes.
I was in this bedroom last week. The walls are green.

8. ¡Caray! ¿Pintaron las paredes? Ahora _____ azules. ¿Quién tomó la decisión de cambiar el color?
Holy moly! They painted the walls? Now they are blue. (... they look blue) Who made the decision to change the color?

9. El edificio al lado del restaurante _____ muy alto.
The building next to the restaurant is very tall.

10. La mayoría de los plásticos _____ duros.
Most plastics are hard.

11. Yo _____ acostado en la cama ahora.
I am lying down in bed now.

12. El almuerzo _____ en la mesa.
The lunch is on the table.

13. Sus abuelos _____ muertos.
Her grandparents are dead.

14. _____ las seis de la mañana.
It is six in the morning.

15. ¿De dónde _____ el Sr. Vásquez?
Where is Mr. Vasquez from?

16. Yo _____ muy cansado. Tengo que viajar a California mañana.
I am very tired. I have to travel to California tomorrow.

17. Tu padre _____ llamándote. Tienes que irte ya.
Your father is calling you. You have to go already.

18. Miguel _____ carpintero en Arizona.
Miguel is a carpenter in Arizona.

19. Ahora _____ en la habitación.
Right now we are in the room.

20. Mi esposa todavía _____ enojada. Me voy a quedar aquí un rato.
My wife is still angry. I am going to stay here a while.

21. Adrián _____ de camerero ahora, pero ya sabemos que _____ traductor.
Adrian is working as a a waiter right now, but we know he was a translator.

22. ¿A cómo _____ la docena de huevos?
How much is a dozen eggs?

23. ¿A cuánto _____ el kilo de zanahorias hoy?
How much is a kilo of carrots today?

24. ¿A cómo _____ el euro en Colombia?
How much is the euro in Colombia?

25. Esta manzana en la canasta _____ negra y podrida. Normalmente, este tipo de manzana _____ rojo.
This apple in the basket is black and rotten. Typically, this type of apple is red.

CHAPTER SIX

Final Review

You've Come A Long Way!—
¡Has Recorrido Un Camino Muy Largo!

Now it's time to see what you're made of. It's been a long hard road, but you made it! You climbed up the the mountain and are close to the top. So how do you feel? By this time, you should feel confident in your understanding of the usages of Ser and Estar. Remember that with practice, we only get better and better. Make sure that you are well rested and you have your cup of coffee at your side before starting this review. So turn to the next page when your ready… It'll be fun!

Side Note: These are the same questions that you have studied throughout the book, but now they are in random order. Be sure to use the proper verb tense and form of Ser or Estar. Refer to the **conjugation charts** of Ser and Estar in the back of the book if you need help.

Now for the final review that will strengthen and confirm our Ser and Estar feelers!

REPASO

Final Review

This review consists of 175 sentences, so go at your own pace, and if your brain starts hurting, take a break! There are no surprises here, since you have seen every one of these sentences throughout the book, and this review will definitely strengthen what you have learned. Don't worry, you will surely do fine after having done all those practice exercises, right? Let's dive in, then.

Fill in the blanks using the correct form of Ser or Estar.

1. Ya aprobé el examen, así que ahora _____ ecuatoriano.
I passed the test, so now I am an Ecuadorian.

2. Estamos de vacaciones en Argentina pero _____ de Chile.
We are on vacation in Argentina but we are from Chile.

3. _____ por comer algo.
I'm in the mood to eat something.

4. El momento que esperábamos _____ al caer.
The moment we were waiting for is about to occur.

5. Sara _____ de buen humor porque acaba de comprar un carro.
Sara is in a good mood because she just bought a car.

6. Emiliano _____ en el limbo después de escuchar la noticia.
Emiliano was feeling lost after hearing the news.

7. Catalina _____ a sus anchas en la casa de su novio.
Catalina was very comfortable in her boyfriend's house.

8. La novia de Lucas _____ fea cuando lleva ese abrigo de piel.
Lucas' girlfriend looks ugly when she wears that fur coat.

9. Esta sopa coreana _____ una sopa fría, porque así se come en Corea del Sur.
This Korean soup is a cold soup because that's how it is eaten in South Korea.

10. Esta es una sopa fría, pero la mesera me la trajo caliente. ¿Por qué _____ caliente la sopa esta vez?
This is a cold soup, but the waitress brought it to me hot. Why is this soup hot this time?

11. Compré esta camisa de lana ayer y _____ grande. La eché a la secadora y mira lo que pasó. Ahora _____ pequeña.
I bought this wool shirt yesterday and it was big. I threw it in the dryer and look what happened. Now it's small.

12. Marina _____ una mujer encantadora y cariñosa, pero cuando fuimos a la tienda anoche, _____ muy enojada.
Marina is a pleasant and affectionate woman, but when we went to the store last night, she was very angry.

13. ¿Y ella, cómo es? Ella _____ bien callada. Siempre ha sido así.
And what is she like? She is really quiet. She's always been like that.

14. Estuve en este dormitorio la semana pasada. Las paredes _____ verdes.
I was in this bedroom last week. The walls are green.

15. ¡Caray! ¿Pintaron las paredes? Ahora _____ azules. ¿Quién tomó la decisión de cambiar el color?
Holy moly! They painted the walls? Now they are blue. (… they look blue) Who made the decision to change the color?

16. Aquel engeniero _____ del país más extenso del

mundo. _____ ruso.

That engineer over there is from the biggest country in he world. He is Russian.

17. Desde que yo era niño, ese anciano ha dicho que _____ danés. Sin embargo, la verdad es que no _____ de Dinamarca.

Since I was a kid, that elderly gentleman has said that he is Danish. Nevertheless, the truth is that he is not from Denmark.

18. El hombre _____ de nacionalidad boliviana.

The man is of Bolivian nationality. (He's Bolivian.)

19. ¿Y tú? ¿Cuál _____ tu raza?

And you? What's your race?

20. Mis amigos que viven en Los Ángeles _____ jardineros paisajistas.

My friends that live in Los Angeles are landscape gardeners.

21. Él trabaja con armas. _____ soldado.

He works with weapons. He is a soldier.

22. El músico pasa su tiempo libre ayudando a otros porque _____ pacifista.

The musician spends his free time helping others because he is a pacifist.

23. Para _____ urólogo, hay que saber mucho sobre la medicina.

To be a urologist, you have to know a lot about medicine.

24. Raúl, según su hermana Carmen, siempre ha _____ gordo y feo.

Raúl, according to his sister Carmen, has always been fat and ugly.

25. Rebeca nunca va a la playa— ella sólo _____ una persona naturalmente bronceada.

Rebecca never goes to the beach— she is just a naturally tanned person.

26. La Señora Madrigal _____ vieja y bizca.
Mrs. Madrigal **is** old and cross-eyed.

27. El niño, que se llama Hernán, _____ pelirrojo.
Pero a él no le gusta porque quisiera tener el pelo moreno.
The boy, who is named Hernán, **is** a read-head. But he doesn't like it because he would like to have dark hair.

28. El atleta del dibujo de arriba _____ fuerte, pero el enano también _____ relativamente fuerte.
The athlete in the drawing above **is** strong, but the dwarf **is** also relatively strong.

29. Sus consejos le ayudaron a enderezar la dirección de la empresa. Él _____ un jefe muy sabio.
His advice helped them straighten out the direction of the company. He is a very wise boss.

30. Alberto _____ presentuoso. Cree que hace todo mejor que nadie.
Alberto is arrogant. He thinks he does everything better than anyone.

31. Ella _____ una mujer muy superficial. Lo que dice me aburre.
She is a very superficial woman. What she says bores me.

32. Te dije que mi primo _____ de poca confiaza y tú no me lo creíste.
I told you that my cousin was untrustworthy and you did not believe me.

33. Donald Trump no es político. Sin embargo, _____ una persona carismática, y lo bueno es que sabe mucho acerca de los negocios.
Donald Trump is not a politician. However, he is a charismatic person, and the good thing is that he knows a lot about business.

34. Francisco _____ muy católico. Algún día quere ser

el Papa.

Francisco is very catholic. Some day he wants to be the Pope.

35. Para algunas personas, el ateísmo se considera una religión. Para _____ ateo, no es necesario creer en un dios.

To some people, atheism is considered a religion. In order to be an atheist, it is not necessary to believe in a god.

36. Ella _____ budista cuando vivía en Corea de Sur pero ahora _____ cristiana.

She was a Buddhist when she lived in South Korea, but now she is a Christian.

37. El niño me preguntó "¿Qué significa creer en Dios, y por qué debo _____ cristiano?"...pero yo no sabía la respuesta.

The boy asked me, "What does it mean to believe in God, and why should I be a Christian? ...but I didn't know the answer.

38. Ellos _____ los musulmanes radicales que vimos ayer en las noticias, los cuales no dejaron a los cristianos sonar las campanas el domingo diciendo que es una falta de respeto a las comunidades musulmanes. No todos los musulmanes son así.

They are the Radical Muslims that we saw on the news yesterday, which did not let the Christians sound their church bells on Sunday, saying that it is a lack of respect to the Muslim communities. Not all Muslims are like that.

39. La forma de la luna en el cielo se llama "círculo". La luna _____ un círculo.

The shape of the moon in the sky is called a "circle". The moon is a circle.

40. La parte superior de la mesa _____ cuadrada.
The top of the table is square.

41. La parte inferior del barco _____ curvo.
The bottom part of the boat is curved.

42. El anillo de plata giró en el aire. El hecho de que el anillo _____ redondo decidió cómo iba a aterrizar.

The silver ring swung in the air. The fact that the ring was round determined how it would land.

43. El trozo de queso _____ triangular.
The piece of cheese was triangular.

44. La niña quiere ser policía cuando _____ grande.
The girl wants to be a police officer when she grows up (when she is big).

45. ¿Cuál es el país más grande del mundo? Rusia _____ el más grande, ¡y _____ demasiado grande!
What is the biggest country in the world. Russia es the biggest, and it's too big!

46. Este celular _____ muy grande para mi mano. ¿Tiene usted otro más pequeño?
This cell phone is very big for my hand. Do you have a smaller one?

47. El agua en este lugar solía _____ muy profundo, pero ya no.
The water in this place used to be very deep, but not anymore.

48. Además, los niveles de pobreza extrema entre los padres solteros en los Estados Unidos _____ de gran tamaño.
Furthermore, levels of deep poverty among single parents in the United States are of great size.

49. El anillo de Jorge _____ de plata.
George's ring is made of silver.

50. Mi casa que se va a construir _____ de ladrillo.
My house that is going to be built will be made of brick.

51. El altavoz _____ de metal, alambres, y un imán.
The speaker is made of metal, wires, and a magnet.

52. El marco _____ de madera y vidrio.

132

The frame is made of wood and glass.

53. Todas las botellas _____ hechas de plástico por los trabajadores de esta fábrica. Así que las botellas _____ de plástico.
All the bottles are made of plastic by the workers in this factory. So the bottles are made of plastic.

54. Este concepto no _____ mío, sino que ha sido acuñado por el Sr. Suárez.
This concept is not mine, but rather has been coined by Mr. Suárez.

55. Mi amado _____ mío, y yo _____ suya.
My beloved is mine, and I am his.

56. Todos los juguetes debajo de la cama _____ de mi cachorro.
All the toys under the bed are my puppy's.

57. La canción popular que le gusta a Amanda se llama "La Fiesta _____ De Nosotros".
The popular song that Amanda likes is called "The Party Is Ours".

58. Mi casa _____ su casa.
My house is your house.

59. Según Álex, _____ músico famoso _____ tener una vida muy ocupada mientras ganas mucho dinero.
According to Alex, being a famous musician is having a really busy life while you earn a lot of money.

60. Beber demasiado alcohol _____ peligroso.
Drinking too much alcohol is dangerous.

61. Aleki me ha dicho que _____ samoano, pero ya no. No creo que eso sea posible.
Aleki told me that he was Samoan, but not anymore. I don't believe that that's possible.

62. No creemos que aquel predicador _____
sudamericano porque su acento parece _____ europeo,
quizás de España.
We do not believe that that preacher over there is South
American because his accent seems to be European, perhaps from
Spain.

63. Los españoles, los canarios, y los andaluces
_____ de la misma etnia.
Spaniards, Canary Islanders and Andalusians are from the
same ethnicity.

64. Personas con raíces africanas, nacidas en el continente
americano, _____ afroamericanas.
Persons with African roots, born in the American continent,
are Afro-Americans.

65. Mi abuelo ha _____ un buen relojero durante la
mayoría de su vida.
My grandfather has been a good watchmaker for most of his
life.

66. _____ estúpido no _____ aconsejable.
Being stupid is not advisable.

67. Disparar un arma _____ un arte en ese país en
ese período.
Shooting a gun was an art in that country during that period.

68. Estudiar este libro _____ algo que te ayudará
mucho con los verbos Ser y Estar.
Studying this book is something that will help you a lot with
the verbs Ser and Estar.

69. Mañana va a _____ mi cumpleaños.
Toworrow's going to be my birthday.

70. Ayer _____ martes.
Yesterday was Tuesday.

71. Ahora _____ la una y media.

Right now it's one thirty.

72. _____ a viernes.
It is Friday.

73. _____ la una y cuarto.
It's 1:15.

74. La mujer está al lado de la niña. La mujer _____ la madre de la niña.
The lady is beside the girl. The lady is the girl's mother.

75. Melodía _____ mi mamá.
Melody is my mother.

76. Luz _____ mi ex-novia.
Luz is my ex-girlfriend.

77. Mi hermana dará luz a un bebé el próximo mes. _____ mi sobrino.
My sister will have a baby next month. He will be my nephew.

78. Mi jefe, José Cambián, es el primo del rey de España.
Mi boss, José Cambián, is the cousin of the king of Spain.

79. Cuando _____ niño, fue mi elección caminar sólo a la escuela.
When I was a child, it was my choice to walk to school alone.

80. _____ una lástima que no existan más posibilidades para tener éxito.
It is a pity that there are not more opportunities to succeed.

81. _____ necesario trabajar duro para vivir bien. Así que eso es lo que hice.
It was necessary to work hard in order to live well. So that is what I did.

82. _____ interesante ver la nueva película.
It is going to be interesting to see the new movie.

83. _____ ridículo que ellos fueran al restaurante esta noche en vez de ir a la boda de su hermana.

It would be ridiculous for them to go to the restaurant tonight instead of going to their sister's wedding.

84. Fue lo que hizo él cuando _____ presidente, hace diez años.

That is what he did when he was presidente 10 years ago.

85. Si _____ presidente de Ecuador ¿cuál sería tu primera decisión?

If you were president of Ecuador, what would be your first decision?

86. Antes de que ganara esa elección, _____ gobernador de Texas durante cuatro años.

Before he won that election, he was governor of Texas for 4 years.

87. Rita Barbera _____ la alcaldesa de Valencia, España entre 1991 y 2015.

Rita Barbera was the mayor of Valencia, Spain from 1991 to 2015.

88. Hay gente que considera al papa una figura política de europea. Sin embargo, no _____ un político sino un líder religioso.

There are those who consider the Pope a political figure. Nevertheless, he is not a politician but rather a religious leader.

89. Esta cantidad de harina _____ suficiente para hacer una torta.

This amount of flour is enough to make a cake.

90. Doce dividido entre tres _____ cuatro.

Twelve divided by three is four.

91. El cuadrado de un número x _____ "x al cuadrado". Se escribe como "$x2$".

The square of a number x is "x squared". It is written as "$x2$".

92. Ellos _____ dos personas distintas.
They are two different people.

93. Tres libras mas una libra _____ igual a cuatro
libras.
Three pounds plus one pound is equal to four pounds.

94. Carlos _____ un buen oficial. Trabaja muy duro.
Carlos is a good officer. He works very hard.

95. Los carros japoneses _____ vehículos muy
populares aquí en los Estados Unidos.
Japanese cars are very popular vehicles here in the United
States.

96. Juan 1:1-2 dice "En el principio era el Verbo y el Verbo
_____ con Dios, y el Verbo _____ Dios."
John 1:1-2 says "In the beginning was the Word and the
Word was with God, and the Word was God."

97. El juguete favorito de Shawna _____ su erizo que
chilla cuando se aprieta.
Shawna's favorite toy is her hedgehog that squeaks when
you squeeze it.

98. La comida favorita de nuestros hijos debe _____
la pizza.
Our kids' favorite food must be pizza.

99. Vosotros _____ inteligentes.
Be smart.

100. No _____ aburrido, profesor. Díganos algo
gracioso. (usted)
Don't be boring, teacher. Tell us something funny.

101. Haz algo bueno. _____ presidente cuando seas
grande. (tú)
Do something good. Be president when you grow up.

102. ! _____ buenos! (ustedes)
You all be good!

103. (Por telefono) Bueno, ¿quién habla? ¡Pedro! ¿Cómo has _____?
(On the phone) Hello. Who is it? Pedro! How have you been?

104. Y tu hermana mayor, ¿Cómo _____ ella?
What about your older sister, how is she?

105. Estamos bien. Y ustedes, ¿Cómo _____?
We're well. (or more commonly: We're good.) And you (all/guys), how are you?

106. He pasado muchas noches sin dormir, pero _____ bien.
I have had many sleepless nights, but I'm fine.

107. ¿Dónde _____ mis guantes?
Where are my gloves?

108. Aunque tú _____ allí, no importa, porque no te dejan entrar.
Even though you are there, it doesn't matter because they don't let you in.

109. La luna _____ muy lejos de la tierra.
The moon is very far from the earth.

110. El partido _____ en el parque donde vimos toda la comida.
The game was in the park where we saw all the food.

111. Siempre que mi tía Beca _____ con nuestra familia, mi tío Adán tiende a enfadarse.
Whenever my aunt Beca is with our family, my uncle Adán tends to get angry.

112. Yo _____ ahora mismo.
I am studying right now.

113. Si te _____, hay que irte ya.
If you are getting angry, you need to leave now.

114. Noemí _____ pantalones azules hoy.
Noemí is wearing blue pants today.

115. Yo sí recibí clases de guitarra cuando _____
niña.
I took guitar classes when I was a girl.

116. Estoy mirando estas tarántulas pequeñas, y es casi
imposible saber quién _____ macho y quién _____
hembra.
I am looking at these small tarantulas and it is almost
impossible to know which is a male and which is a female.

117. La mujer se enfadó y dijo en voz alta "¡Si yo
_____ hombre vosotros me habríais dado este trabajo!"
The woman got angry and said aloud "If I were a man you
would have given me this job!"

118. ¿Te importa si el médico _____ hombre o mujer?
Bueno, pues.
Do you care whether the doctor is a man or a woman? Okay,
then.

119. ¿En dólares cuánto _____?
How much would it be in dollars?

120. El amor no _____ barato. Cuesta mucho... y a
veces, demasiado.
Love is not cheap. It costs a lot... and at times, too much.

121. El juez te dirá cuánto _____ el valor de la multa.
The judge will tell you the amount of the fine. (The judge will
tell you how much the amount of the fine is.)

122. ¿Compraste un coche nuevo? ¿Cuánto _____?
You bought a new car? How much was it?

123. Quisiera saber cuánto _____ este libro con el descuento. Sale a €9.55.

I would like to know how much this book will be with the discount. It comes out to €9.55.

124. _____ importante saber leer porque te ayudará mucho durante tu vida.

It is important to know how to read because it will help you a lot throughout your life.

125. Raquel _____ al lado del niño para que aprenda.

Raquel is painting alongside the boy so that he can learn.

126. Más vale que te _____ para salir. Vamos a llegar tarde.

You'd better be getting ready to leave. We're going to be late.

127. Marta _____ triste después del funeral. Ahora _____ mejor.

Marta was sad after the funeral. Now she is better.

128. A Samuel le dio cuenta de que su perro _____ enfermo.

Samuel realized that his dog was sick.

129. Ella _____ contenta porque su hija le trajo un dibujo que hizo en la escuela.

She is happy because her daughter brought her a drawing that she made in school.

130. Eliezer _____ bien vestido esta noche, ¿no?

Eliezer is well dressed tonight, isn't he?

131. La novia de Rogelio, Lisa, _____ celosa ayer porque Amanda, quien es muy bella, vino a visitarlo y se quedó en su casa durante dos horas.

Rogelio's girlfriend, Lisa, was jealous yesterday because Amanda, who is very beautiful, came to visit him and she stayed at his house for two hours.

132. Carlos y Lupe _____ casados.
Carlos and Lupe are married.

133. Felipe ya no _____ un hombre soltero, porque ahora se casó. _____ casado.
Felipe is no longer a single man because he got married. He is married.

134. El marido de Luz falleció el año pasado. Luz _____ viuda.
Luz's husband passed away last year. Luz is widowed.

135. Un hombre que _____ soltero no _____ casado.
A man who is single is not married.

136. Hay que hacer todo lo que podamos mientras _____ vivos.
We have to do all we can while we are alive.

137. El profesor se enojó. Él _____ enojado ahora.
The teacher got mad. He is angry now.

138. Los estudiantes se levantaron del piso. Ahora ellos _____ de pie.
The students got up from the floor. Now they are standing.

139. El gato se estiró en el sofá. El gato _____ estirado en el sofá.
The cat stretched out on the couch. The cat is stretched out on the couch.

140. Paré el coche al ver el perro. El coche _____ parado.
I stopped the care when I saw the dog. The car was stopped.

141. El autor escribió un libro de gramática española. El libro _____ escrito. El libro _____ escrito por el autor.
The author wrote a book on Spanish grammar. The book was written. The book was written by the author.

142. _____ de acuerdo.
Let's agree.

143. No _____ enfermos mañana. Es muy importante que no lleguéis tarde, también. (vosotros)
Don't be sick tomorrow. It's very important that you don't arrive late, also.

144. _____ ustedes preparados para defender sus fronteras.
Be prepared to defend your borders.

145. Por nada _____ afanosos.
Be anxious for nothing. (vosotros)

146. _____ tú aquí a las cinco en punto.
Be here at five o'clock.

147. El edificio al lado del restaurante _____ muy alto.
The building next to the restaurant is very tall.

148. La mayoría de los plásticos _____ duros.
Most plastics are hard.

149. Yo _____ acostado en la cama ahora.
I am lying down in bed now.

150. El almuerzo _____ en la mesa.
The lunch is on the table.

151. Sus abuelos _____ muertos.
Her grandparents are dead.

152. _____ las seis de la mañana.
It is six in the morning.

153. ¿De dónde _____ el Sr. Vásquez?
Where is Mr. Vasquez from?

154. Yo _____ muy cansado. Tengo que viajar a

California mañana.
I am very tired. I have to travel to California tomorrow.

155. Tu padre _____ llamándote. Tienes que irte ya.
Your father is calling you. You have to go already.

156. Miguel _____ carpintero en Arizona.
Miguel is a carpenter in Arizona.

157. Ahora _____ en la habitación.
Right now we are in the room.

158. Mi esposa todavía _____ enojada. Me voy a
quedar aquí un rato.
My wife is still angry. I am going to stay here a while.

159. Adrián _____ de camerero ahora, pero ya
sabemos que _____ traductor.
Adrian is working as a a waiter right now, but we know he
was a translator.

160. ¿A cómo _____ la docena de huevos?
How much is a dozen eggs?

161. ¿A cuánto _____ el kilo de zanahorias hoy?
How much is a kilo of carrots today?

162. ¿A cómo _____ el euro en Colombia?
How much is the euro in Colombia?

163. Esta manzana en la canasta _____ negra y
podrida. Normalmente, este tipo de manzana normalmente
_____ rojo.
This apple in the basket **is** black and rotten. Typically, this
type of apple **is** normally red.

164. Su abuela _____ española.
His grandmother was Spanish.

165. Nosotros _____ en el partido.
We were at the game.

166. Nuestros papás _____ de Guatemala.
Our parents were from Guatemala.

167. Nosotros _____ allí dos días.
We were there for two days.

168. _____ un día muy divertido.
It was a very fun day.

169. El concierto _____ en el Teatro de Luz mañana a las seis en punto. (ser/estar)
The concert will be at the Teatro de Luz tomorrow at six o'clock sharp.

170. La computadora _____ sobre el escritorio. (ser/estar)
The computer is on the desk.

171. La boda _____ en la sala de conferencia de ese edificio.(ser/estar)
The wedding will be in the conference hall of that building.

172. El vestido que la novia va a usar _____ en la sala de conferencia de ese edificio. (ser/estar)
The dress that the bride is going to use is in the conference hall of that building.

173. El juego de fútbol _____ en el estadio que _____ en el centro de la ciudad. (ser/estar)
The soccer game will be held in the stadium that is in the center of the city.

174. No _____ malagradecidos con vuestra abuela. (vosotros)
Do not be ungrateful to your grandmother.

175. ¡Yo _____ estupendamente!

I'm doing great!

CHAPTER SEVEN

Perfecting Your Spanish

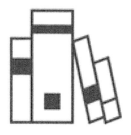

Perfecting Your Spanish Language Skills

Practice makes perfect. You've probably heard this phrase thousands of times over. We will never actually be perfect, but I believe we can get pretty close if we really put our minds to it.

There are many methods and systems for mastering any foreign language, and not every one of them is going to work for everybody. We have to find out *what works for us*, sometimes through trial and error. We can boil all of these methods and systems down to six points that, in my own experience, are tremendously important:

1. **Reading**

2. **Writing**

3. **Listening**

4. **Producing (Speaking)**

5. **Getting Feedback**

6. **Translating**

Reading

If we are going to become fluent in Spanish, we'll need to spend time reading it. Just like reading in English helps us (or whatever your native language may be), reading in Spanish will help us become more comfortable with the vocabulary and grammar "ins and outs" that will allow us to express what we are thinking. Just being able to see the words and ideas as we are reading reinforces our memory of those words for the future.

1. Read books, the news, or anything else in Spanish on a daily basis. You can read the news on-line, obtain your favorite books in Spanish (especially if you have already read them in English). It is now very easy to find inexpensive, and often free, ebooks online.

2. Reading expands your vocabulary— and what's more, by reading and coming across the same words over and over, the words become reinforced in our minds and are easily recalled when we need to use them again. Reading makes the words "stick". If you come across a word you don't know, highlight it and keep on reading. Later on, you can look up these words. You'll surely encounter these same words as you continue reading. Don't let unknown vocabulary slow down your reading. Think about it, did it slow you down when you had a limited vocabulary as a child? Nope, you probably just ignored that difficult word and continued on. Sooner or later, you learned the word and you remembered it easily the next time you encountered it.

3. Read silently (to yourself). When you do this, you will become a faster reader, because you will learn to recognize what the Spanish words look like (you'll recognize their shape) and how they stand out against the rest of the words around them.

4. Read out loud at a slow pace to practice and improve pronunciation. Speed will come with time and lots of practice.

5. Read a book while listening to its accompanying audio, if available. This method will greatly help improve your listing skills and will help you to associate the written word with spoken word.

Writing

If we are planning to become fluent in Spanish, it is also extremely helpful if we write in Spanish. I mentioned this at the beginning of the book, with emphasis on writing out the sentences in the exercises. Sure, we can learn a language without writing, as some people have. But writing down what we are learning will tremendously improve our recognition of Spanish words and sentence structure, and will hugely speed up the language learning process.

Writing reinforces what you are learning. What's more, if you practice writing Spanish while you learn, you will undoubtedly expand your Spanish vocabulary.

1. So, whenever you have Spanish exercises to do, take the time to write them out in your notebook.

2. Making a grocery list? Write it down in Spanish.

3. Download a messaging app, such as HelloTalk or iTalki and use your phone to find native Spanish speakers around the world that are learning English— and help each other learn while you message each other.

4. Find an article or story that you like, in Spanish, and copy it down on paper.

5. I recommend handwriting as opposed to typing. There is a correlation between writing and our ability to remember. We should use it to our advantage.

Listening

Listening to Spanish is very important. As we discussed previously, reading out loud and listening to audiobooks tremendously help us to associate the words with the sounds. There are all kinds of ways we can listen to Spanish to improve our skills: Movies, TV, YouTube videos, music, podcasts, audiobooks, anything in Spanish.

1. Passive listening is helpful in training our ears to the sounds of Spanish. The more we listen, the more it becomes familiar to us, and not so foreign.

2. Active listening, in my experience, is extremely helpful in our quest to become fluent in Spanish. We can listen to Spanish while thinking about what exactly we are hearing. We can try to pick out the different words, analyzing when words, phrases and sentences begin, and where they end. By listening actively, we train our ears to recognize all the various interjections, statements, and questions. We can hear the intonation of the language— the rise and fall of the pitch of the speaker's voice. Through active listening, we can listen for the accent in each word. This reinforces the memory of our Spanish vocabulary.

3. Something that can be very helpful in improving listening and comprehension is pausing the audio, then summarizing in Spanish what we've just heard. This allows us to *think* better in Spanish, which in turn enables us to improve our listening skills.

Speaking

In order to *produce the language,* we must speak. There is no negotiating. We *need to speak* in order to improve our pronunciation. It involves improving our *prosody,* which is the patterns of stress and intonation in a language, and our *accent,* which is producing the sounds of Spanish correctly.

1. *Shadowing.* An American professor, Alexander Arguelles, developed a technique called "Shadowing". While listening to a language, in our case, Spanish, you attempt to repeat, or *shadow,* what you are hearing at the same speed as the audio. Professor Arguelles emphasizes that it is most beneficial to shadow while walking briskly to ensure alertness. I personally have found shadowing while walking kind of annoying, but if it works for you, go for it! Everyone learns better in their own way. I actually find it easier to use this method while driving. Glossika.com has some excellent audio material that I have used for this.

2. *Speak at a steady rhythm.* When we speak Spanish, we may have a tendency to try to speak too fast in attempt to mimic a native speaker. If we are not at the native speaker level yet, we are bound to fumble around and things just won't come out correctly. That being said, we don't need to speak really slowly or anything, but rather speak at a steady, comfortable speed. Take your time and get the words out. The listener will understand if he or she knows we are not a native Spanish speaker.

3. Talk to yourself in Spanish. This one's easy. We can do this in the car or walking around the house. There is no way this cannot improve our speaking skills— because we are speaking!

4. Think in Spanish. Whatever we do, if we *try* to think it in Spanish, we *train* ourselves to think in Spanish. This, in turn, will help us later on to produce Spanish on demand, allowing for better word flow.

Getting Feedback

Feedback is a very important part of language learning. Of course, we can actually study on our own, speak on our own, and therefore progress on our own, but actually conversing in real-life with another human, preferably a native Spanish speaker, can be immensely helpful. While practicing conversation, our "language partner" can take notes on what you say— things you need to improve on, whether it be bad grammar and syntax, wrong vocabulary, or anything else. At the end of the session, your language partner can give you feedback that will be invaluable to your Spanish language learning journey.

Translating

Translating text back and forth between English and Spanish is very valuable in that it *makes us think*. When we translate words, sentences and paragraphs, it exposes us to new words and phrases and will help in the future when we attempt to speak the language with someone.

Make sure you translate text that is interesting to you. Translate articles relating to your line of work, your hobbies, places you've been, etc. Then, when you meet a native Spanish speaker, you will be able to speak about yourself and your interests with ease.

ANSWERS

ANSWERS TO EXERCISES

 Exercise 1— Placement Test.

1. No me gustan los platos de papel. Me gusta este plato porque **es** de cerámica.
I don't like paper plates. I like this plate because it's made of ceramic.

2. Corea del Sur **es** el lugar más interesante que he visitado.
South Korea is the most interesting place that I have visited.

3. El profesor de matemáticas **es** muy aburrido. No me gusta su clase.
The math teacher es very boring. I don't like his class.

4. ¿Cuál **es** el primer auto que compraste?
What's the first car that you bought?

5. El concierto va a **ser** en el parque mañana por la tarde. ¿Vas a ir?
The concert is going to be at the park tomorrow evening. Are you going?

6. No. Él no asiste a una iglesia judía. **Es** católico.
No. He doesn't attend a Jewish church. He's Catholic.

7. Mi hermana mayor **es** una persona bien lista.
My big sister is a very smart person.

8. Fui a clase ayer. Yo **estuve** tan aburrido que tuve que dejar la clase.
I went to class yesterday. I was so bored that I had to leave the class.

9. Voy a comprar todo esto. ¿Cuánto **es**? ¿Y a cuánto **está** un kilo de carne de res hoy?
I am going to buy all this. How much is it (the total)? And how much is a kilo of beef going for today?

10. ¿Si pudieras **ser** una persona famosa por un día, a quién elegirías?
If you could be a famous person for one day, who would you chose?

11. Yo **estoy** a punto de salir a correr.
I am about to go out to run.

12. El jefe quería que yo **estuviera** en el trabajo a las seis de la mañana el día siguiente.
The boss wanted me to be at work at six in the morning the following day.

13. Alejandro, aunque tú **estés** enfermo, vas a ir a la escuela hoy.
Alejandro, even though you are sick, you are going to go to school today.

14. La cuchara grande que **es** de plástico **está** allí.
The big plastic spoon is over there. (the spoon made of plastic)

15. Si tuvieras mil millones de dólares **serías** rico.
If you had a billion dollars, you would be rich.

Exercise 2.

1. Su abuela era española.
His grandmother was Spanish.

2. Nosotros estábamos en el partido.
We were at the game.

3. Nuestros papás eran de Guatemala.
Our parents were from Guatemala.

4. Nosotros estuvimos allí dos días.
We were there for two days.

5. Fue un día muy divertido.
It was a very fun day.

Exercise 3.

1. Ya aprobé el examen, así que ahora soy ecuatoriano.
I passed the test, so now I am an Ecuadorian.

2. Estamos de vacaciones en Argentina pero somos de Chile.
We are on vacation in Argentina but we are from Chile.

3. Aquel engeniero es del país más extenso del mundo. es ruso.
That engineer over there is from the biggest country in he world. He is Russian.

4. Desde que yo era niño, ese anciano ha dicho que es danés. Sin embargo, la verdad es que no es de Dinamarca.
Since I was a kid, that elderly gentleman has said that he is

Danish. Nevertheless, the truth is that he is not from Denmark.

5. El hombre es de nacionalidad boliviana.
The man is of Bolivian nationality. (He's Bolivian.)

 Exercise 4.

1. ¿Y tú? ¿Cuál es tu raza?
And you? What's your race?

2. Aleki me ha dicho que era samoano, pero ya no. No creo que eso sea posible.
Aleki told me that he was Samoan, but not anymore. I don't believe that that's possible.

3. No creemos que aquel predicador sea sudamericano porque su acento parece ser europeo, quizás de España.
We do not believe that that preacher over there is South American because his accent seems to be European, perhaps from Spain.

4. Los españoles, los canarios, y los andaluces son de la misma etnia.
Spaniards, Canary Islanders and Andalusians are from the same ethnicity.

5. Personas con raíces africanas, nacidas en el continente americano, son afroamericanas.
Persons with African roots, born in the American continent, are Afro-Americans.

 Exercise 5.

1. Mi abuelo ha sido un buen relojero durante la mayoría de

su vida.
My grandfather has been a good watchmaker for most of his life.

2. Mis amigos que viven en Los Ángeles son jardineros paisajistas.
My friends that live in Los Angeles are landscape gardeners.

3. Él trabaja con armas. Es soldado.
He works with weapons. He is a soldier.

4. El músico pasa su tiempo libre ayudando a otros porque es pacifista.
The musician spends his free time helping others because he is a pacifist.

5. Para ser urólogo, hay que saber mucho sobre la medicina.
To be a urologist, you have to know a lot about medicine

 Exercise 6.

1. Raúl, según su hermana Carmen, siempre ha sido gordo y feo.
Raúl, according to his sister Carmen, has always been fat and ugly.

2. Rebeca nunca va a la playa— ella sólo es una persona naturalmente bronceada.
Rebecca never goes to the beach— she is just a naturally tanned person

3. La Señora Madrigal es vieja y bizca.
Mrs. Madrigal is old and cross-eyed.

4. El niño, que se llama Hernán, es pelirrojo. Pero a él no le gusta porque quisiera tener el pelo moreno.
The boy, who is named Hernán, is a read-head. But he

doesn't like it because he would like to have dark hair.

5. El atleta del dibujo de arriba es fuerte, pero el enano también es relativamente fuerte.
The athlete in the drawing above is strong, but the dwarf is also relatively strong.

 Exercise 7.

1. Sus consejos le ayudaron a enderezar la dirección de la empresa. Él es un jefe muy sabio.
His advice helped them straighten out the direction of the company. He is a very wise boss.

2. Alberto es presentuoso. Cree que hace todo mejor que nadie.
Alberto is arrogant. He thinks he does everything better than anyone.

3. Ella es una mujer muy superficial. Lo que dice me aburre.
She is a very superficial woman. What she says bores me.

4. Te dije que mi primo era de poca confiaza y tú no me lo creíste.
I told you that my cousin was untrustworthy and you did not believe me.

5. Donald Trump no es político. Sin embargo, es una persona carismática, y lo bueno es que sabe mucho acerca de los negocios.
Donald Trump is not a politician. However, he is a charismatic person, and the good thing is that he knows a lot about business.

Exercise 8.

1. Francisco es muy católico. Algún día quere ser el Papa.
Francisco is very catholic. Some day he wants to be the Pope.

2. Para algunas personas, el ateísmo se considera una religión. Para ser ateo, no es necesario creer en un dios.
To some people, atheism is considered a religion. In order to be an atheist, it is not necessary to believe in a god.

3. Ella era budista cuando vivía en Corea de Sur pero ahora es cristiana.
She was a Buddhist when she lived in South Korea, but now she is a Christian.

4. El niño me preguntó "¿Qué significa creer en Dios, y por qué debo ser cristiano?"...pero yo no sabía la respuesta.
The boy asked me, "What does it mean to believe in God, and why should I be a Christian? ...but I didn't know the answer.

5. Ellos son los musulmanes radicales que vimos ayer en las noticias, los cuales no dejaron a los cristianos sonar las campanas el domingo diciendo que es una falta de respeto a las comunidades musulmanes. No todos los musulmanes son así.
They are the Radical Muslims that we saw on the news yesterday, which did not let the Christians sound their church bells on Sunday, saying that it is a lack of respect to the Muslim communities. Not all Muslims are like that.

 Exercise 9.

1. La forma de la luna en el cielo se llama "círculo". La luna es un círculo.

The shape of the moon in the sky is called a "circle". The moon is a circle.

2. La parte superior de la mesa es cuadrada.
The top of the table is square.

3. La parte inferior del barco es curvo.
The bottom part of the boat is curved.

4. El anillo de plata giró en el aire. El hecho de que el anillo fuera redondo decidió cómo iba a aterrizar.
The silver ring swung in the air. The fact that the ring was round determined how it would land.

5. El trozo de queso era triangular.
The piece of cheese was triangular.

 Exercise 10.

1. La niña quiere ser policía cuando sea grande.
The girl wants to be a police officer when she grows up (when she is big).

2. ¿Cuál es el país más grande del mundo? Rusia es el más grande, ¡y es demasiado grande!
What is the biggest country in the world. Russia es the biggest, and it's too big!

3. Este celular es muy grande para mi mano. ¿Tiene usted otro más pequeño?
This cell phone is very big for my hand. Do you have a smaller one?

4. El agua en este lugar solía ser muy profundo, pero ya no.
The water in this place used to be very deep, but not anymore.

5. Además, los niveles de pobreza extrema entre los padres

solteros en los Estados Unidos son de gran tamaño.

Furthermore, levels of deep poverty among single parents in the United States are of great size.

 Exercise 11.

1. El anillo de Jorge es de plata.
George's ring is made of silver.

2. Mi casa que se va a construir será de ladrillo.
My house that is going to be built will be made of brick.

3. El altavoz es de metal, alambres, y un imán.
The speaker is made of metal, wires, and a magnet.

4. El marco es de madera y vidrio.
The frame is made of wood and glass.

5. Todas las botellas están hechas de plástico por los trabajadores de esta fábrica. Así que las botellas son de plástico.
All the bottles are made of plastic by the workers in this factory. So the bottles are made of plastic

 Exercise 12.

1. Este concepto no es mío, sino que ha sido acuñado por el Sr. Suárez.
This concept is not mine, but rather has been coined by Mr. Suárez.

2. Mi amado es mío, y yo soy suya.
My beloved is mine, and I am his.

3. Todos los juguetes debajo de la cama son de mi cachorro.

All the toys under the bed are my puppy's.

4. La canción popular que le gusta a Amanda se llama "La Fiesta Es De Nosotros".
The popular song that Amanda likes is called "The Party Is Ours".

5. Mi casa es su casa.
My house is your house.

 Exercise 13.

1. Según Álex, ser músico famoso es tener una vida muy ocupada mientras ganas mucho dinero.
According to Alex, being a famous musician is having a really busy life while you earn a lot of money.

2. Beber demasiado alcohol es peligroso.
Drinking too much alcohol is dangerous.

3. Ser estúpido no es aconsejable.
Being stupid is not advisable.

4. Disparar un arma era un arte en ese país en ese período.
Shooting a gun was an art in that country during that period.

5. Estudiar este libro es algo que te ayudará mucho con los verbos Ser y Estar.
Studying this book is something that will help you a lot with the verbs Ser and Estar.

 Exercise 14.

1. Mañana va a ser mi cumpleaños.

Toworrow's going to be my birthday.

2. Ayer fue martes.
Yesterday was Tuesday.

3. Ahora es la una y media.
Right now it's one thirty.

4. Estamos a viernes.
It is Friday.

5. Es la una y cuarto.
It's 1:15.

 Exercise 15.

1. La mujer está al lado de la niña. La mujer es la madre de la niña.
The lady is beside the girl. The lady is the girl's mother.

2. Melodía es mi mamá.
Melody is my mother.

3. Luz es mi ex-novia.
Luz is my ex-girlfriend.

4. Mi hermana dará luz a un bebé el próximo mes. Será mi sobrino.
My sister will have a baby next month. He will be my nephew.

5. Mi jefe, José Cambián, es el primo del rey de España.
Mi boss, José Cambián, is the cousin of the king of Spain.

Exercise 16.

1. El concierto será en el Teatro de Luz mañana a las seis en punto.
The concert will be at the Teatro de Luz tomorrow at six o'clock sharp.

2. La computadora está sobre el escritorio.
The computer is on the desk.

3. La boda será en la sala de conferencia de ese edificio.
The wedding will be in the conference hall of that building.

4. El vestido que la novia va a usar está en la sala de conferencia de ese edificio.
The dress that the bride is going to use is in the conference hall of that building.

5. El juego de fútbol será en el estadio que está en el centro de la ciudad.
The soccer game will be held in the stadium that is in the center of the city.

 Exercise 17.

1. Cuando era niño, fue mi elección caminar sólo a la escuela.
When I was a child, it was my choice to walk to school alone.

2. Yo sí recibí clases de guitarra cuando era niña.
I took guitar classes when I was a girl.

3. Estoy mirando estas tarántulas pequeñas, y es casi imposible saber quién es macho y quién es hembra.

I am looking at these small tarantulas and it is almost impossible to know which is a male and which is a female.

4. La mujer se enfadó y dijo en voz alta "¡Si yo fuera hombre vosotros me habríais dado este trabajo!"
The woman got angry and said aloud "If I were a man you would have given me this job!"

5. ¿Te importa si el médico es hombre o mujer? Bueno, pues.
Do you care whether the doctor is a man or a woman? Okay, then.

 Exercise 18.

1. ¿En dólares cuánto sería?
How much would it be in dollars?

2. El amor no es barato. Cuesta mucho… y a veces, demasiado.
Love is not cheap. It costs a lot… and at times, too much.

3. El juez te dirá cuánto es el valor de la multa.
The judge will tell you the amount of the fine. (The judge will tell you how much the amount of the fine is.)

4. ¿Compraste un coche nuevo? ¿Cuánto fue?
You bought a new car? How much was it?

5. Quisiera saber cuánto será este libro con el descuento. Sale a €9.55.
I would like to know how much this book will be with the discount. It comes out to €9.55.

Exercise 19.

1. Es importante saber leer porque te ayudará mucho durante tu vida.
It is important to know how to read because it will help you a lot throughout your life.

2. Es una lástima que no existan más posibilidades para tener éxito.
It is a pity that there are not more opportunities to succeed.

3. Era necesario trabajar duro para vivir bien. Así que eso es lo que hice.
It was necessary to work hard in order to live well. So that is what I did.

4. Va a ser interesante ver la nueva película.
It is going to be interesting to see the new movie.

5. Sería ridículo que ellos fueran al restaurante esta noche en vez de ir a la boda de su hermana.
It would be ridiculous for them to go to the restaurant tonight instead of going to their sister's wedding.

Exercise 20.

1. Fue lo que hizo él cuando era presidente, hace diez años.
That is what he did when he was presidente 10 years ago.

2. Si fueras presidente de Ecuador ¿cuál sería tu primera decisión?
If you were president of Ecuador, what would be your first decision?

3. Antes de que ganara esa elección, fue gobernador de Texas durante cuatro años.

Before he won that election, he was governor of Texas for 4 years.

4. Rita Barbera fue la alcaldesa de Valencia, España entre 1991 y 2015.

Rita Barbera was the mayor of Valencia, Spain from 1991 to 2015.

5. Hay gente que considera al papa una figura política de europea. Sin embargo, no es un político sino un líder religioso.

There are those who consider the Pope a political figure. Nevertheless, he is not a politician but rather a religious leader.

 Exercise 21.

1. Esta cantidad de harina es suficiente para hacer una torta.

This amount of flour is enough to make a cake.

2. Doce dividido entre tres son cuatro.
Twelve divided by three is four.

3. El cuadrado de un número x es "x al cuadrado". Se escribe como "x2".

The square of a number x is "x squared". It is written as "x2".

4. Ellos son dos personas distintas.
They are two different people.

5. Tres libras mas una libra es igual a cuatro libras.
Three pounds plus one pound is equal to four pounds.

Exercise 22.

1. Carlos es un buen oficial. Trabaja muy duro.
Carlos is a good officer. He works very hard.

2. Los carros japoneses son vehículos muy populares aquí en los Estados Unidos.
Japanese cars are very popular vehicles here in the United States.

3. Juan 1:1-2 dice "En el principio era el Verbo y el Verbo estaba con Dios, y el Verbo era Dios."
John 1:1-2 says "In the beginning was the Word and the Word was with God, and the Word was God."

4. El juguete favorito de Shawna es su erizo que chilla cuando se aprieta.
Shawna's favorite toy is her hedgehog that squeaks when you squeeze it.

5. La comida favorita de nuestros hijos debe ser la pizza.
Our kids' favorite food must be pizza.

Exercise 23.

1. Vosotros sed inteligentes.
Be smart.

2. No sea aburrido, profesor. Díganos algo gracioso.
Don't be boring, teacher. Tell us something funny.

3. Haz algo bueno. Sé presidente cuando seas grande.
Do something good. Be president when you grow up.

4. !Sean buenos! (ustedes)
You all be good!

5. No seáis malagradecidos con vuestra abuela.
Do not be ungrateful to your grandmother.

 Exercise 24.

1. ¡Yo estoy estupendamente!
I'm doing great!

2. (Por telefono) Bueno, ¿quién habla? ¡Pedro! ¿Cómo has estado?
(On the phone) Hello. Who is it? Pedro! How have you been?

3. Y tu hermana mayor, ¿Cómo está ella?
What about your older sister, how is she?

4. Estamos bien. Y ustedes, ¿Cómo están?
We're well. (or more commonly: We're good.) And you (all/guys), how are you?

5. He pasado muchas noches sin dormir, pero estoy bien.
I have had many sleepless nights, but I'm fine.

 Exercise 25.

1. ¿Dónde están mis guantes?
Where are my gloves?

2. Aunque tú estés allí, no importa, porque no te dejan entrar.
Even though you are there, it doesn't matter because they

don't let you in.

3. La luna está muy lejos de la tierra.
The moon is very far from the earth.

4. El partido fue en el parque donde vimos toda la comida.
The game was in the park where we saw all the food.

5. Siempre que mi tía Beca esté con nuestra familia, mi tío Adán tiende a enfadarse.
Whenever my aunt Beca is with our family, my uncle Adán tends to get angry.

 Exercise 26.

1. Yo estoy estudiando ahora mismo.
I am studying right now.

2. Si te estás enfadando, hay que irte ya.
If you are getting angry, you need to leave now.

3. Noemí está llevando pantalones azules hoy.
Noemí is wearing blue pants today.

4. Raquel está pintando al lado del niño para que aprenda.
Raquel is painting alongside the boy so that he can learn.

5. Más vale que te estés preparando para salir. Vamos a llegar tarde.
You'd better be getting ready to leave. We're going to be late.

Exercise 27.

1. Marta estaba triste después del funeral. Ahora está mejor.
Marta was sad after the funeral. Now she is better.

2. A Samuel le dio cuenta de que su perro estaba enfermo.
Samuel realized that his dog was sick.

3. Ella está contenta porque su hija le trajo un dibujo que hizo en la escuela.
She is happy because her daughter brought her a drawing that she made in school.

4. Eliezer está bien vestido esta noche, ¿no?
Eliezer is well dressed tonight, isn't he?

5. La novia de Rogelio, Lisa, estaba celosa ayer porque Amanda, quien es muy bella, vino a visitarlo y se quedó en su casa durante dos horas.
Rogelio's girlfriend, Lisa, was jealous yesterday because Amanda, who is very beautiful, came to visit him and she stayed at his house for two hours.

Exercise 28.

1. Carlos y Lupe están casados.
Carlos and Lupe are married.

2. Felipe ya no es un hombre soltero, porque ahora se casó. Está casado.
Felipe is no longer a single man because he got married. He is married.

3. El marido de Luz falleció el año pasado. Luz está viuda.

Luz's husband passed away last year. Luz is widowed.

4. Un hombre que está soltero no está casado.
A man who is single is not married.

5. Hay que hacer todo lo que podamos mientras estamos
vivos.
We have to do all we can while we are alive.

 Exercise 29.

1. El profesor se enojó. Él está enojado ahora.
The teacher got mad. He is angry now.

2. Los estudiantes se levantaron del piso. Ahora ellos están
de pie.
The students got up from the floor. Now they are standing.

3. El gato se estiró en el sofá. El gato está estirado en el
sofá.
The cat stretched out on the couch. The cat is stretched out
on the couch.

4. Paré el coche al ver el perro. El coche estaba parado.
I stopped the care when I saw the girl. The car was stopped.

5. El autor escribió un libro de gramática española. El libro
está escrito. El libro fue escrito por el autor.
The author wrote a book on Spanish grammar. The book
was written. The book was written by the author.

 Exercise 30.

1. Estemos de acuerdo.

Let's agree.

2. No estéis enfermos mañana. Es muy importante que no lleguéis tarde, también.
Don't be sick tomorrow. It's very important that you don't arrive late, also.

3. Estén ustedes preparados para defender sus fronteras.
Be prepared to defend your borders.

4. Por nada estéis afanosos.
Be anxious for nothing.

5. Está tú aquí a las cinco en punto.
Be here at five o'clock.

 Exercise 31.

1. Estoy por comer algo.
I'm in the mood to eat something.

2. El momento que esperábamos está al caer.
The moment we were waiting for is about to occur.

3. Sara está de buen humor porque acaba de comprar un carro.
Sara is in a good mood because she just bought a car.

4. Emiliano estaba en el limbo después de escuchar la noticia.
Emiliano was feeling lost after hearing the news.

5. Catalina estaba a sus anchas en la casa de su novio.
Catalina was very comfortable in her boyfriend's house.

Exercise 32.

1. La novia de Lucas está fea cuando lleva ese abrigo de piel.
Lucas' girlfriend looks ugly when she wears that fur coat.

2. Esta sopa coreana es una sopa fría, porque así se come en Corea del Sur.
This Korean soup is a cold soup because that's how it is eaten in South Korea.

3. Esta es una sopa fría, pero la mesera me la trajo caliente. ¿Por qué está caliente la sopa esta vez?
This is a cold soup, but the waitress brought it to me hot. Why is this soup hot this time?

4. Compré esta camisa de lana ayer y era grande. La eché a la secadora y mira lo que pasó. Ahora está pequeña.
I bought this wool shirt yesterday and it was big. I threw it in the dryer and look what happened. Now it's small.

5. Marina es una mujer encantadora y cariñosa, pero cuando fuimos a la tienda anoche, estaba muy enojada.
Marina is a pleasant and affectionate woman, but when we went to the store last night, she was very angry.

6. ¿Y ella, cómo es? Ella es bien callada. Siempre ha sido así.
And what is she like? She is really quiet. She's always been like that.

7. Estuve en este dormitorio la semana pasada. Las paredes son verdes.
I was in this bedroom last week. The walls are green.

8. ¡Caray! ¿Pintaron las paredes? Ahora están azules.

¿Quién tomó la decisión de cambiar el color?

Holy moly! They painted the walls? Now they are blue. (… they look blue) Who made the decision to change the color?

9. El edificio al lado del restaurante es muy alto.
The building next to the restaurant is very tall.

10. La mayoría de los plásticos son duros.
Most plastics are hard.

11. Yo estoy acostado en la cama ahora.
I am lying down in bed now.

12. El almuerzo está en la mesa.
The lunch is on the table.

13. Sus abuelos están muertos.
Her grandparents are dead.

14. Son las seis de la mañana.
It is six in the morning.

15. ¿De dónde es el Sr. Vásquez?
Where is Mr. Vasquez from?

16. Yo estoy muy cansado. Tengo que viajar a California mañana.
I am very tired. I have to travel to California tomorrow.

17. Tu padre está llamándote. Tienes que irte ya.
Your father is calling you. You have to go already.

18. Miguel es carpintero en Arizona.
Miguel is a carpenter in Arizona.

19. Ahora estamos en la habitación.
Right now we are in the room.

20. Mi esposa todavía está enojada. Me voy a quedar aquí un rato.
My wife is still angry. I am going to stay here a while.

21. Adrián está de camarero ahora, pero ya sabemos que es traductor.

Adrian is working as a a waiter right now, but we know he was a translator.

22. ¿A cómo está la docena de huevos?
How much is a dozen eggs?

23. ¿A cuánto está el kilo de zanahorias hoy?
How much is a kilo of carrots today?

24. ¿A cómo está el euro en Colombia?
How much is the euro in Colombia?

25. Esta manzana en la canasta está negra y podrida. Normalmente, este tipo de manzana es rojo.

This apple in the basket is black and rotten. Typically, this type of apple is red.

Answers to Final Review

1. Ya aprobé el examen, así que ahora soy ecuatoriano.
I passed the test, so now I am an Ecuadorian.

2. Estamos de vacaciones en Argentina pero somos de Chile.
We are on vacation in Argentina but we are from Chile.

3. Estoy por comer algo.
I'm in the mood to eat something.

4. El momento que esperábamos está al caer.
The moment we were waiting for is about to occur.

5. Sara está de buen humor porque acaba de comprar un carro.
Sara is in a good mood because she just bought a car.

6. Emiliano estaba en el limbo después de escuchar la noticia.
Emiliano was feeling lost after hearing the news.

7. Catalina estaba a sus anchas en la casa de su novio.
Catalina was very comfortable in her boyfriend's house.

8. La novia de Lucas está fea cuando lleva ese abrigo de piel.

Lucas' girlfriend looks ugly when she wears that fur coat.

9. Esta sopa coreana es una sopa fría, porque así se come en Corea del Sur.
This Korean soup is a cold soup because that's how it is eaten in South Korea.

10. Esta es una sopa fría, pero la mesera me la trajo caliente. ¿Por qué está caliente la sopa esta vez?
This is a cold soup, but the waitress brought it to me hot. Why is this soup hot this time?

11. Compré esta camisa de lana ayer y era grande. La eché a la secadora y mira lo que pasó. Ahora está pequeña.
I bought this wool shirt yesterday and it was big. I threw it in the dryer and look what happened. Now it's small.

12. Marina es una mujer encantadora y cariñosa, pero cuando fuimos a la tienda anoche, estaba muy enojada.
Marina is a pleasant and affectionate woman, but when we went to the store last night, she was very angry.

13. ¿Y ella, cómo es? Ella es bien callada. Siempre ha sido así.
And what is she like? She is really quiet. She's always been like that.

14. Estuve en este dormitorio la semana pasada. Las paredes son verdes.
I was in this bedroom last week. The walls are green.

15. ¡Caray! ¿Pintaron las paredes? Ahora están azules. ¿Quién tomó la decisión de cambiar el color?
Holy moly! They painted the walls? Now they are blue. (… they look blue) Who made the decision to change the color?

16. Aquel engeniero es del país más extenso del mundo. es ruso.
That engineer over there is from the biggest country in he world. He is Russian.

17. Desde que yo era niño, ese anciano ha dicho que es danés. Sin embargo, la verdad es que no es de Dinamarca.
Since I was a kid, that elderly gentleman has said that he is Danish. Nevertheless, the truth is that he is not from Denmark.

18. El hombre es de nacionalidad boliviana.
The man is of Bolivian nationality. (He's Bolivian.)

19. ¿Y tú? ¿Cuál es tu raza?
And you? What's your race?

20. Mis amigos que viven en Los Ángeles son jardineros paisajistas.
My friends that live in Los Angeles are landscape gardeners.

21. Él trabaja con armas. Es soldado.
He works with weapons. He is a soldier.

22. El músico pasa su tiempo libre ayudando a otros porque es pacifista.
The musician spends his free time helping others because he is a pacifist.

23. Para ser urólogo, hay que saber mucho sobre la medicina.
To be a urologist, you have to know a lot about medicine.

24. Raúl, según su hermana Carmen, siempre ha sido gordo y feo.
Raúl, according to his sister Carmen, has always been fat and ugly.

25. Rebeca nunca va a la playa— ella sólo es una persona naturalmente bronceada.
Rebecca never goes to the beach— she is just a naturally tanned person.

26. La Señora Madrigal es vieja y bizca.
Mrs. Madrigal is old and cross-eyed.

27. El niño, que se llama Hernán, es pelirrojo. Pero a él no

le gusta porque quisiera tener el pelo moreno.

The boy, who is named Hernán, is a read-head. But he doesn't like it because he would like to have dark hair.

28. El atleta del dibujo de arriba es fuerte, pero el enano también es relativamente fuerte.

The athlete in the drawing above is strong, but the dwarf is also relatively strong.

29. Sus consejos le ayudaron a enderezar la dirección de la empresa. Él es un jefe muy sabio.

His advice helped them straighten out the direction of the company. He is a very wise boss.

30. Alberto es presentuoso. Cree que hace todo mejor que nadie.

Alberto is arrogant. He thinks he does everything better than anyone.

31. Ella es una mujer muy superficial. Lo que dice me aburre.

She is a very superficial woman. What she says bores me.

32. Te dije que mi primo era de poca confiaza y tú no me lo creíste.

I told you that my cousin was untrustworthy and you did not believe me.

33. Donald Trump no es político. Sin embargo, es una persona carismática, y lo bueno es que sabe mucho acerca de los negocios.

Donald Trump is not a politician. However, he is a charismatic person, and the good thing is that he knows a lot about business.

34. Francisco es muy católico. Algún día quere ser el Papa.

Francisco is very catholic. Some day he wants to be the Pope.

35. Para algunas personas, el ateísmo se considera una religión. Para ser ateo, no es necesario creer en un dios.

To some people, atheism is considered a religion. In order to be an atheist, it is not necessary to believe in a god.

36. Ella era budista cuando vivía en Corea de Sur pero ahora es cristiana.
She was a Buddhist when she lived in South Korea, but now she is a Christian.

37. El niño me preguntó "¿Qué significa creer en Dios, y por qué debo ser cristiano?"…pero yo no sabía la respuesta.
The boy asked me, "What does it mean to believe in God, and why should I be a Christian? …but I didn't know the answer.

38. Ellos son los musulmanes radicales que vimos ayer en las noticias, los cuales no dejaron a los cristianos sonar las campanas el domingo diciendo que es una falta de respeto a las comunidades musulmanes. No todos los musulmanes son así.
They are the Radical Muslims that we saw on the news yesterday, which did not let the Christians sound their church bells on Sunday, saying that it is a lack of respect to the Muslim communities. Not all Muslims are like that.

39. La forma de la luna en el cielo se llama "círculo". La luna es un círculo.
The shape of the moon in the sky is called a "circle". The moon is a circle.

40. La parte superior de la mesa es cuadrada.
The top of the table is square.

41. La parte inferior del barco es curvo.
The bottom part of the boat is curved.

42. El anillo de plata giró en el aire. El hecho de que el anillo fuera redondo decidió cómo iba a aterrizar.
The silver ring swung in the air. The fact that the ring was round determined how it would land.

43. El trozo de queso era triangular.
The piece of cheese was triangular.

44. La niña quiere ser policía cuando sea grande.
The girl wants to be a police officer when she grows up (when she is big).

45. ¿Cuál es el país más grande del mundo? Rusia es el más grande, ¡y es demasiado grande!
What is the biggest country in the world. Russia es the biggest, and it's too big!

46. Este celular es muy grande para mi mano. ¿Tiene usted otro más pequeño?
This cell phone is very big for my hand. Do you have a smaller one?

47. El agua en este lugar solía ser muy profundo, pero ya no.
The water in this place used to be very deep, but not anymore.

48. Además, los niveles de pobreza extrema entre los padres solteros en los Estados Unidos son de gran tamaño.
Furthermore, levels of deep poverty among single parents in the United States are of great size.

49. El anillo de Jorge es de plata.
George's ring is made of silver.

50. Mi casa que se va a construir será de ladrillo.
My house that is going to be built will be made of brick.

51. El altavoz es de metal, alambres, y un imán.
The speaker is made of metal, wires, and a magnet.

52. El marco es de madera y vidrio.
The frame is made of wood and glass.

53. Todas las botellas están hechas de plástico por los trabajadores de esta fábrica. Así que las botellas son de plástico.
All the bottles are made of plastic by the workers in this factory. So the bottles are made of plastic.

54. Este concepto no es mío, sino que ha sido acuñado por el Sr. Suárez.
This concept is not mine, but rather has been coined by Mr. Suárez.

55. Mi amado es mío, y yo soy suya.
My beloved is mine, and I am his.

56. Todos los juguetes debajo de la cama son de mi cachorro.
All the toys under the bed are my puppy's.

57. La canción popular que le gusta a Amanda se llama "La Fiesta Es De Nosotros".
The popular song that Amanda likes is called "The Party Is Ours".

58. Mi casa es su casa.
My house is your house.

59. Según Álex, ser músico famoso es tener una vida muy ocupada mientras ganas mucho dinero.
According to Alex, being a famous musician is having a really busy life while you earn a lot of money.

60. Beber demasiado alcohol es peligroso.
Drinking too much alcohol is dangerous.

61. Aleki me ha dicho que era samoano, pero ya no. No creo que eso sea posible.
Aleki told me that he was Samoan, but not anymore. I don't believe that that's possible.

62. No creemos que aquel predicador sea sudamericano porque su acento parece ser europeo, quizás de España.
We do not believe that that preacher over there is South American because his accent seems to be European, perhaps from Spain.

63. Los españoles, los canarios, y los andaluces son de la misma etnia.

Spaniards, Canary Islanders and Andalusians are from the same ethnicity.

64. Personas con raíces africanas, nacidas en el continente americano, son afroamericanas.
Persons with African roots, born in the American continent, are Afro-Americans.

65. Mi abuelo ha sido un buen relojero durante la mayoría de su vida.
My grandfather has been a good watchmaker for most of his life.

66. Ser estúpido no es aconsejable.
Being stupid is not advisable.

67. Disparar un arma era un arte en ese país en ese período.
Shooting a gun was an art in that country during that period.

68. Estudiar este libro es algo que te ayudará mucho con los verbos Ser y Estar.
Studying this book is something that will help you a lot with the verbs Ser and Estar.

69. Mañana va a ser mi cumpleaños.
Toworrow's going to be my birthday.

70. Ayer fue martes.
Yesterday was Tuesday.

71. Ahora es la una y media.
Right now it's one thirty.

72. Estamos a viernes.
It is Friday.

73. Es la una y cuarto.
It's 1:15.

74. La mujer está al lado de la niña. La mujer es la madre de

la niña.
The lady is beside the girl. The lady is the girl's mother.

75. Melodía es mi mamá.
Melody is my mother.

76. Luz es mi ex-novia.
Luz is my ex-girlfriend.

77. Mi hermana dará luz a un bebé el próximo mes. Será mi sobrino.
My sister will have a baby next month. He will be my nephew.

78. Mi jefe, José Cambián, es el primo del rey de España.
Mi boss, José Cambián, is the cousin of the king of Spain.

79. Cuando era niño, fue mi elección caminar sólo a la escuela.
When I was a child, it was my choice to walk to school alone.

80. Es una lástima que no existan más posibilidades para tener éxito.
It is a pity that there are not more opportunities to succeed.

81. Era necesario trabajar duro para vivir bien. Así que eso es lo que hice.
It was necessary to work hard in order to live well. So that is what I did.

82. Va a ser interesante ver la nueva película.
It is going to be interesting to see the new movie.

83. Sería ridículo que ellos fueran al restaurante esta noche en vez de ir a la boda de su hermana.
It would be ridiculous for them to go to the restaurant tonight instead of going to their sister's wedding.

84. Fue lo que hizo él cuando era presidente, hace diez años.
That is what he did when he was presidente 10 years ago.

85. Si fueras presidente de Ecuador ¿cuál sería tu primera decisión?
If you were president of Ecuador, what would be your first decision?

86. Antes de que ganara esa elección, fue gobernador de Texas durante cuatro años.
Before he won that election, he was governor of Texas for 4 years.

87. Rita Barbera fue la alcaldesa de Valencia, España entre 1991 y 2015.
Rita Barbera was the mayor of Valencia, Spain from 1991 to 2015.

88. Hay gente que considera al papa una figura política de europea. Sin embargo, no es un político sino un líder religioso.
There are those who consider the Pope a political figure. Nevertheless, he is not a politician but rather a religious leader.

89. Esta cantidad de harina es suficiente para hacer una torta.
This amount of flour is enough to make a cake.

90. Doce dividido entre tres son cuatro.
Twelve divided by three is four.

91. El cuadrado de un número x es "x al cuadrado". Se escribe como "$x2$".
The square of a number x is "x squared". It is written as "$x2$".

92. Ellos son dos personas distintas.
They are two different people.

93. Tres libras mas una libra es igual a cuatro libras.
Three pounds plus one pound is equal to four pounds.

94. Carlos es un buen oficial. Trabaja muy duro.

Carlos is a good officer. He works very hard.

95. Los carros japoneses son vehículos muy populares aquí en los Estados Unidos.
Japanese cars are very popular vehicles here in the United States.

96. Juan 1:1-2 dice "En el principio era el Verbo y el Verbo estaba con Dios, y el Verbo era Dios."
John 1:1-2 says "In the beginning was the Word and the Word was with God, and the Word was God."

97. El juguete favorito de Shawna es su erizo que chilla cuando se aprieta.
Shawna's favorite toy is her hedgehog that squeaks when you squeeze it.

98. La comida favorita de nuestros hijos debe ser la pizza.
Our kids' favorite food must be pizza.

99. Vosotros sed inteligentes.
Be smart.

100. No sea aburrido, profesor. Díganos algo gracioso.
Don't be boring, teacher. Tell us something funny.

101. Haz algo bueno. Sé presidente cuando seas grande.
Do something good. Be president when you grow up.

102. !Sean buenos! (ustedes)
You all be good!

103. (Por telefono) Bueno, ¿quién habla? ¡Pedro! ¿Cómo has estado?
(On the phone) Hello. Who is it? Pedro! How have you been?

104. Y tu hermana mayor, ¿Cómo está ella?
What about your older sister, how is she?

105. Estamos bien. Y ustedes, ¿Cómo están?

We're well. (or more commonly: We're good.) And you (all/guys), how are you?

106. He pasado muchas noches sin dormir, pero estoy bien.
I have had many sleepless nights, but I'm fine.

107. ¿Dónde están mis guantes?
Where are my gloves?

108. Aunque tú estés allí, no importa, porque no te dejan entrar.
Even though you are there, it doesn't matter because they don't let you in.

109. La luna está muy lejos de la tierra.
The moon is very far from the earth.

110. El partido fue en el parque donde vimos toda la comida.
The game was in the park where we saw all the food.

111. Siempre que mi tía Beca esté con nuestra familia, mi tío Adán tiende a enfadarse.
Whenever my aunt Beca is with our family, my uncle Adán tends to get angry.

112. Yo estoy estudiando ahora mismo.
I am studying right now.

113. Si te estás enfadando, hay que irte ya.
If you are getting angry, you need to leave now.

114. Noemí está llevando pantalones azules hoy.
Noemí is wearing blue pants today.

115. Yo sí recibí clases de guitarra cuando era niña.
I took guitar classes when I was a girl.

116. Estoy mirando estas tarántulas pequeñas, y es casi imposible saber quién es macho y quién es hembra.
I am looking at these small tarantulas and it is almost impossible to know which is a male and which is a female.

117. La mujer se enfadó y dijo en voz alta "¡Si yo fuera hombre vosotros me habríais dado este trabajo!"
The woman got angry and said aloud "If I were a man you would have given me this job!"

118. ¿Te importa si el médico es hombre o mujer? Bueno, pues.
Do you care whether the doctor is a man or a woman? Okay, then.

119. ¿En dólares cuánto sería?
How much would it be in dollars?

120. El amor no es barato. Cuesta mucho… y a veces, demasiado.
Love is not cheap. It costs a lot… and at times, too much.

121. El juez te dirá cuánto es el valor de la multa.
The judge will tell you the amount of the fine. (The judge will tell you how much the amount of the fine is.)

122. ¿Compraste un coche nuevo? ¿Cuánto fue?
You bought a new car? How much was it?

123. Quisiera saber cuánto será este libro con el descuento. Sale a €9.55.
I would like to know how much this book will be with the discount. It comes out to €9.55.

124. Es importante saber leer porque te ayudará mucho durante tu vida.
It is important to know how to read because it will help you a lot throughout your life.

125. Raquel está pintando al lado del niño para que aprenda.
Raquel is painting alongside the boy so that he can learn.

126. Más vale que te estés preparando para salir. Vamos a llegar tarde.

You'd better be getting ready to leave. We're going to be late.

127. Marta estaba triste después del funeral. Ahora está mejor.

Marta was sad after the funeral. Now she is better.

128. A Samuel le dio cuenta de que su perro estaba enfermo.

Samuel realized that his dog was sick.

129. Ella está contenta porque su hija le trajo un dibujo que hizo en la escuela.

She is happy because her daughter brought her a drawing that she made in school.

130. Eliezer está bien vestido esta noche, ¿no?

Eliezer is well dressed tonight, isn't he?

131. La novia de Rogelio, Lisa, estaba celosa ayer porque Amanda, quien es muy bella, vino a visitarlo y se quedó en su casa durante dos horas.

Rogelio's girlfriend, Lisa, was jealous yesterday because Amanda, who is very beautiful, came to visit him and she stayed at his house for two hours.

132. Carlos y Lupe están casados.

Carlos and Lupe are married.

133. Felipe ya no es un hombre soltero, porque ahora se casó. Está casado.

Felipe is no longer a single man because he got married. He is married.

134. El marido de Luz falleció el año pasado. Luz está viuda.

Luz's husband passed away last year. Luz is widowed.

135. Un hombre que está soltero no está casado.

A man who is single is not married.

136. Hay que hacer todo lo que podamos mientras estamos vivos.
We have to do all we can while we are alive.

137. El profesor se enojó. Él está enojado ahora.
The teacher got mad. He is angry now.

138. Los estudiantes se levantaron del piso. Ahora ellos están de pie.
The students got up from the floor. Now they are standing.

139. El gato se estiró en el sofá. El gato está estirado en el sofá.
The cat stretched out on the couch. The cat is stretched out on the couch.

140. Paré el coche al ver el perro. El coche estaba parado.
I stopped the care when I saw the girl. The car was stopped.

141. El autor escribió un libro de gramática española. El libro está escrito. El libro fue escrito por el autor.
The author wrote a book on Spanish grammar. The book was written. The book was written by the author.

142. Estemos de acuerdo.
Let's agree.

143. No estéis enfermos mañana. Es muy importante que no lleguéis tarde, también.
Don't be sick tomorrow. It's very important that you don't arrive late, also.

144. Estén ustedes preparados para defender sus fronteras.
Be prepared to defend your borders.

145. Por nada estéis afanosos.
Be anxious for nothing.

146. Está tú aquí a las cinco en punto.
Be here at five o'clock.

147. El edificio al lado del restaurante es muy alto.
The building next to the restaurant is very tall.

148. La mayoría de los plásticos son duros.
Most plastics are hard.

148. Yo estoy acostado en la cama ahora.
I am lying down in bed now.

150. El almuerzo está en la mesa.
The lunch is on the table.

151. Sus abuelos están muertos.
Her grandparents are dead.

152. Son las seis de la mañana.
It is six in the morning.

153. ¿De dónde es el Sr. Vásquez?
Where is Mr. Vasquez from?

154. Yo estoy muy cansado. Tengo que viajar a California mañana.
I am very tired. I have to travel to California tomorrow.

155. Tu padre está llamándote. Tienes que irte ya.
Your father is calling you. You have to go already.

156. Miguel es carpintero en Arizona.
Miguel is a carpenter in Arizona.

157. Ahora estamos en la habitación.
Right now we are in the room.

158. Mi esposa todavía está enojada. Me voy a quedar aquí un rato.
My wife is still angry. I am going to stay here a while.

159. Adrián está de camerero ahora, pero ya sabemos que es traductor.
Adrian is working as a a waiter right now, but we know he

was a translator.

160. ¿A cómo está la docena de huevos?
How much is a dozen eggs?

161. ¿A cuánto está el kilo de zanahorias hoy?
How much is a kilo of carrots today?

162. ¿A cómo está el euro en Colombia?
How much is the euro in Colombia?

163. Esta manzana en la canasta está negra y podrida. Normalmente, este tipo de manzana es rojo.
This apple in the basket is black and rotten. Typically, this type of apple is red.

164. Su abuela era española.
His grandmother was Spanish.

165. Nosotros estábamos en el partido.
We were at the game.

166. Nuestros papás eran de Guatemala.
Our parents were from Guatemala.

167. Nosotros estuvimos allí dos días.
We were there for two days.

168. Fue un día muy divertido.
It was a very fun day.

169. El concierto será en el Teatro de Luz mañana a las seis en punto.
The concert will be at the Teatro de Luz tomorrow at six o'clock sharp.

170. La computadora está sobre el escritorio.
The computer is on the desk.

171. La boda será en la sala de conferencia de ese edificio.
The wedding will be in the conference hall of that building.

172. El vestido que la novia va a usar está en la sala de conferencia de ese edificio.

The dress that the bride is going to use is in the conference hall of that building.

173. El juego de fútbol será en el estadio que está en el centro de la ciudad.

The soccer game will be held in the stadium that is in the center of the city.

174. No seáis malagradecidos con vuestra abuela.
Do not be ungrateful to your grandmother.

175. ¡Yo estoy estupendamente!
I'm doing great!

CONJUGATIONS OF SER & ESTAR

SER, CONJUGATED

nfinitive: ser
Gerund: siendo
Past Participle: sido

Perfect Infinitive: haber sido
Perfect Gerund: habiendo sido

Indicative

	Present	**Perfect**
yo	soy	he sido
tú	eres	has sido
él/ella/Ud.	es	ha sido
nosotros	somos	hemos sido
vosotros	sois	habéis sido
Ellos/ellas/Uds.	son	han sido

	Imperfect	**Pluperfect**
yo	era	había sido
tú	eras	habías sido
él/ella/Ud.	era	habían sido
nosotros	éramos	habíamos sido
vosotros	erais	habíais sido
ellos/ellas/Uds.	eran	habían sido

Preterite	**Past Anterior**

197

yo	fui	hube sido
tú	fuiste	hubiste sido
él/ella/Ud.	fue	hubo sido
nosotros	fuimos	hubimos sido
vosotros	fuisteis	hubisteis sido
ellos/ellas/Uds.	fueron	hubieron sido

	Future	**Future Perfect**
yo	seré	habré sido
tú	serás	habrás sido
él/ella/Ud.	será	habrá sido
nosotros	seremos	habremos sido
vosotros	seréis	habréis sido
ellos/ellas/Uds.	serán	habrán sido

	Conditional	**Conditional Perfect**
yo	sería	habría sido
tú	serías	habrías sido
él/ella/Ud.	sería	habría sido
nosotros	seríamos	habríamos sido
vosotros	seríais	habríais sido
ellos/ellas/Uds.	serían	habrían sido

Subjunctive

	Present	**Perfect**
yo	sea	haya sido
tú	seas	hayas sido
él/ella/Ud.	sea	haya sido
nosotros	seamos	hayamos sido
vosotros	seáis	hayáis sido
ellos/ellas/Uds.	sean	hayan sido

	Imperfect I	**Pluperfect I**

yo	fuera	hubiera sido
tú	fueras	hubieras sido
él/ella/Ud.	fuera	hubiera sido
nosotros	fuéramos	hubiéramos sido
vosotros	fuerais	hubierais sido
ellos/ellas/Uds.	fueran	hubieran sido

	Imperfect II	**Pluperfect II**
yo	fuese	hubiese sido
tú	fueses	hubieses sido
él/ella/Ud.	fuese	hubiese sido
nosotros	fuésemos	hubiésemos sido
vosotros	fueseis	hubieseis sido
ellos/ellas/Uds.	fuesen	hubiesen sido

Imperative

	Affirmative	**Negative**
yo	—	—
tú	sé	no seas
él/ella/Ud.	sea	no sea
nosotros	seamos	no seamos
vosotros	sed	no seáis
ellos/ellas/Uds.	sean	no sean

ESTAR, CONJUGATED

Infinitive: estar
Gerund: estando

Past Participle: estado

Perfect Infinitive: haber estado
Perfect Gerund: habiendo estado

Indicative

	Present	Perfect
yo	estoy	he estado
tú	estás	has estado
él/ella/Ud.	está	ha estado
nosotros	estamos	hemos estado
vosotros	estáis	habéis estado
Ellos/ellas/Uds.	están	han estado

	Imperfect	Pluperfect
yo	estaba	había estado
tú	estabas	habías estado
él/ella/Ud.	estaba	había estado
nosotros	estábamos	habíamos estado
vosotros	estabais	habíais estado
ellos/ellas/Uds.	estaban	habían estado

	Preterite	Past Anterior

yo	estuve	hube estado
tú	estuviste	hubiste estado
él/ella/Ud.	estuvo	hubo estado
nosotros	estuvimos	hubimos estado
vosotros	estuvisteis	hubisteis estado
ellos/ellas/Uds.	estuvieron	hubieron estado

| | **Future** | **Future Perfect** |

yo	estaré	habré estado
tú	estarás	habrás estado
él/ella/Ud.	estará	habrá estado
nosotros	estaremos	habremos estado
vosotros	estaréis	habréis estado
ellos/ellas/Uds.	estarán	habrán estado

| | **Conditional** | **Conditional Perfect** |

yo	estaría	habría estado
tú	estarías	habrías estado
él/ella/Ud.	estaría	habría estado
nosotros	estaríamos	habríamos estado
vosotros	estaríais	habríais estado
ellos/ellas/Uds.	estarían	habrían estado

Subjunctive

| | **Present** | **Perfect** |

yo	esté	haya estado
tú	estés	hayas estado
él/ella/Ud.	esté	haya estado
nosotros	estemos	hayamos estado
vosotros	estéis	hayáis estado
ellos/ellas/Uds.	estén	hayan estado

| | **Imperfect I** | **Pluperfect I** |

yo	estuviera	hubiera estado
tú	estuvieras	hubieras estado
él/ella/Ud.	estuviera	hubiera estado
nosotros	estuviéramos	hubiéramos estado
vosotros	estuvierais	hubierais estado
ellos/ellas/Uds.	estuvieran	hubieran estado

	Imperfect II	Pluperfect II
yo	estuviese	hubiese estado
tú	estuvieses	hubieses estado
él/ella/Ud.	estuviese	hubiese estado
nosotros	estuviésemos	hubiésemos estado
vosotros	estuvieseis	hubieseis estado
ellos/ellas/Uds.	estuviesen	hubiesen estado

Imperative

	Affirmative	Negative
yo	—	—
tú	está	no estés
él/ella/Ud.	esté	no esté
nosotros	estemos	no estemos
vosotros	estad	no estéis
ellos/ellas/Uds.	estén	no estén

Printed in Great Britain
by Amazon

80730639R00119